CW00484885

You've go
from **CHINA!**

You've got mail ...
from CHINA!

Hazy Days and Crazy Bites

Martyn Habgood

霍马汀

Huo Ma Ding

THE CHOIR PRESS

First published in the UK in 2013 by The Choir Press

ISBN 978-1-909300-09-5

Foreword

I hope the following e-mails from China over a twelve-year period will give readers an insight into the life of a typical English manager plunged into a completely alien environment and culture. Although in the early days I sent several relatively short e-mails to individual family members and friends, they developed into general e-mails to many friends and colleagues and began to include various photos to add flavour to the stories. During this period rapid changes were taking place in China and these were coupled to my own developing understanding of the country, people and language. These aspects come through in the e-mails as China becomes more westernised and I become more comfortable with my life in China. All of the stories are totally true and I hope you find reading them both enlightening and enjoyable.

Acknowledgements

David and Brian for giving me the first opportunity in China.

Jessie and William who ensured I appreciated the Chinese way of getting things done and stopped me from making mistakes early on.

My assistants, Karen, Matata, Lily, Daisy, Cara, Casey, Echo and Nola, who helped me both at work and with my domestic arrangements.

Many others who have helped and supported me along the way, including:

Geoff, Steve, Andrew, Mark, Jon, Jude, John, Austen, Ian and Jayne.

The many Chinese colleagues who have made my life in China easier than it otherwise might have been, including:

Paul Quan, Claude Yang, Judy Zhao, Lao Yang, Jane Bai, Jaly Zhang, Yin Yu, John Shen, Thomas Wong, Lei Hong and Sun Gang.

Tony and Jenny for their encouragement during the early stages of putting this book together.

Not forgetting my family for putting up with my endless stories and dodgy gifts from China.

Finally, to Miles and Rachel at The Choir Press for enabling this work to be published.

Introduction

It was Sunday 5th November 2006 that I began my journey to a place called Liuzhou in southern China. I was to be the General Manager of a new acquisition by a large British company wishing to expand into the world's fastest-growing economy. I didn't know it at the time but this was to be the start of a wonderful adventure which has kept me enthralled for over five years. A period of my life where I have not only experienced both the highs and lows of my business career, but I have also grown as a person, more than able to survive in this different culture.

Since leaving corporate employment in 2002 I started working as an Interim Manager, taking various assignments with companies that for various reasons were not able or willing to appoint a permanent manager. I found that I really enjoyed the challenge of joining a business with particular problems, focussing on those issues without really having to worry about the politics involved in career progression. Typically I worked with businesses of around 300 employees manufacturing engineered products which were sold throughout the world. As Interim General Manager or Managing Director I was responsible for all functions although particular assignments would require different functional priorities.

It was while I was working for one business in the UK, part of an international group with manufacturing plants in many countries, that my boss, the Group Managing Director, approached me. "We are trying to acquire a business in China which we expect to be the main production facility for the group," he said. "We would like you to go in as General Manager for a few months to manage the transition from a State-owned Chinese company to a business in line with our standards of efficiencies, product quality, health and safety, profitability and growth. Are you interested?"

I have always relished a challenge and this seemed to offer not only a lot of normal business problems but also put into the context of a completely different culture and language, therefore a very interesting opportunity that I found impossible to turn down. All I really knew at the time, even with a lot of background reading, was that this business of 800 people, based in Guangxi province in Southern China, had been run down over several years by the State-owned parent company. The photographs and the financial reports did not look good! I agreed to the challenge but had to wait a few months whilst the negotiations were concluded.

The call finally came in November 2006, so I sorted out my visa, packed a suitcase, said goodbyes to family and friends and flew to China. The business is based in a city called Liuzhou, population three million, a two-hour flight from Hong Kong followed by a two-hour drive to the city of Liuzhou (pronounced Leo Joe).

I stayed in Liuzhou for eight months and together with four other ex-pats and a largely supportive Chinese team rapidly undertook the many tasks to significantly improve the business. I handed over to a new General Manager in mid-2007 and returned to the UK. However it has to be said that the experience was one of the most interesting in the whole of my career and I looked forward to returning for another 'Chinese challenge'. Early in 2008 I had another opportunity to return to Liuzhou, to the same business, but this time to steer it through a period of sales and production growth rather than sort out the wrongs of the previous owners. Later in 2008 I handed over to a permanent Chinese General Manager. Over the next ten years I undertook three more lengthy assignments in different parts of China; my understanding of Chinese culture and my language skills improved to the point where I was completely comfortable living and travelling in this wonderful country.

In 2015 I decided to move into a part-time advisory role for the businesses in China, with regular weekly conference calls from the UK to the local General Manager and travelling to China for two weeks every couple of months to give on-site support.

The following pages attempt to give a flavour of my time and experiences in China, primarily through my e-mails home to friends and family, which with time transformed to regular e-mails to many people to keep them up-to-date with my situation. I have also included various photographs to help visualize my experience.

My Employers

During the first two assignments in China from 2006 to 2008 I was working for GKN PLC, a large British engineering company with businesses throughout the world, primarily aimed at the automotive, aerospace and agricultural markets. GKN had nine other businesses in China and had a well proven strategy of putting ex-pats in for the first 12-18 months to ensure the business complied with GKN standards, then recruiting local Chinese management to run the company. The new acquisition in Liuzhou manufactured wheels for the automotive, mining and crane markets.

The third assignment during 2010 and 2011 saw me working for another well-known British engineering company: David Brown Industrial Gears. Over more than 100 years David Brown had gone from making tractors and owning Aston Martin (the DB marque being David Brown) to focusing on industrial gearboxes and some other precision products. The growth of renewable energy products and public transport in China gave David Brown the opportunity to join forces with an established Chinese company who were already producing complete wind turbines and rail transport products. A joint venture was formed to design and manufacture gearboxes for these markets.

The fourth assignment from mid-2011 to mid-2012 was working for another British engineering company, Bridon Wire Ropes, a long-established international business with several companies throughout the world. The Chinese business started as a joint venture in 2008 and was finally fully purchased in 2010, but performance had begun to deteriorate over several months and there were questions raised about its overall viability.

In 2013 I was appointed General Manager for two embryonic businesses in Chengdu, Sichuan Province, manufacturing parts for MRI scanners. These companies were part of the Medical Division of Avingtrans PLC, a specialist engineering business with a good record of targeted investment and development.

I am extremely grateful for the opportunities and support that these companies and their management teams gave me, without which my life would have been far less exciting. I should also thank my wife Julie and my daughters Becky and Amy for their understanding during my extended months away from home.

The First Session

A New Challenge ... Help!

Based in the city of Liuzhou in Guangxi Province, which is in the central south of China. Although Liuzhou has its own airport, which has a daily flight to Shanghai but not much else, the nearest 'international' airport is Guilin, which is a two-hour drive from Liuzhou but does have a few flights to and from Hong Kong.

E-mails, November 2006 to June 2007

HELLO FROM CHINA – 25th November 2006

Ni Hao (hello),

This is my first attempt to send a picture, so I hope it works. The picture was taken at the opening ceremony on 16th November and shows Brian and David (GKN Bosses) plus my new 'best mate' Mr Huang and myself in our rather fetching beige and blue uniforms. Mr Huang is the recently deposed General Manager who has made way for me, so is not a particularly happy bunny. At this stage we do not know what or who he knows so we are treading carefully and have given him the role of Special Adviser to the General Manager ensuring that he will not lose face. It is custom in China to have a 'Lion Dance' at openings etc. so there were prancing lions and beating drums for what seemed hours warding off the evil spirits. In fact we have two huge concrete lions either side of the factory gate. The opening was a really good day with lots of speeches to the 800ish employees and guests, plus a lot of locals who stopped by to see what was going on. I tried out a bit of Chinese in my speech and got an applause/laugh! There followed a tug-o-war competition with teams from all the different departments, the winners of that knock-out stage having to compete with the 'big nose' team. (The Chinese term for Europeans/Americans is big noses, so I fit in quite well!) Anyway we won, or they let us win as we were the new employers.

Since then it's been pretty tough, I've not had a day off yet, there's lots of health and safety issues and customer quality problems.

Unfortunately there isn't one aspect which I can look at and say "that's good", apart from the attitude of most of the workers. Still it was always going to be a challenge!

I have been given a Chinese name; Huo Ma Ding. Huo is the surname and is the name of an ancient poet, Ma Ding sounds a bit like Martyn but actually means horse (Ma) little river (Ding). So I'm now a bit of a poetic wet horse! I'll get business cards made with English on one side and Chinese, including my Chinese name, on the other.

2

On a positive note the hotel is good and I'm really enjoying most of the food so I'll probably not lose the fat I was hoping to. I've even found some chocolate ice-cream!

Hope you're all keeping well, not long now until I come home for Christmas.

Best Wishes
Martyn Huo Ma Ding

Old and new bosses

Tug-o-war fun!

STILL IN CHINA – 10th December 2006

Hi,

I worked yesterday (Saturday) from 9 till 2.00pm. All visitors are gone now so there's just William and me in town. William is the Brit who's lived out here for 10 years so he's just like a native, his family (wife and 2 boys in their early teens) moved back to the UK last year but they are all coming out to China over Christmas. He lives in a different hotel in the town centre and has lots of Chinese friends through the local church. I slept OK last night thanks to some wine and have just had breakfast. It's got incredibly cold here over the last few days and I've only got a couple of thin pullovers so I'm wearing lots of layers. The maid has just come in to clean the room. I'm going out for a walk along the river this morning and will meet William and our Sales Manager for lunch to talk over a couple of problems we've got with two important customers. Later I've got to prepare a presentation for my trip to Shanghai. I fly up there late tomorrow morning (a two and a half hour flight), meet up with some of the other GKN China managers in the evening and go to one of the factories on Tuesday for the meeting. I hope I can find time to do some Shanghai shopping and get some things (English choccy?) that are not available in Liuzhou. The Big Bosses of GKN China will fly back with me on Wednesday morning and stay until Thursday. So most of next week is taken up with PR activity!!

The offices and meeting rooms are always adorned with pot plants and a lady comes into my office every other day to water my 3 pot plants. When I asked how this all worked I was taken to the back of the factory site behind one of the most dilapidated old buildings where I was shown a large cottage garden growing lots of flowering plants and vegetables. In fact we employ 3 people to manage this. I'm sure this is the only part of the business making a profit at the moment because they sell the veg to other local companies, and no doubt take a cut for themselves. With everything else going on it's not a priority at the moment but I wonder what other under-cover businesses are operating right under our noses?

I'm really looking forward to coming home, only 12 days to go!!

Best wishes

The garden centre at the rear of the factory.

MESSAGE TO MC – 18th December 2006

How very good to hear from you. I trust you are enjoying your life of leisure while some of us toil in the most arduous conditions to repatriate a few sovereigns just to keep you pensioners in the style to which you have become accustomed. That nice Mr Gordon Brown certainly takes such a big chunk that I'm not sure whether this is worth the pain! Anyway you'll be pleased to know that the workforce do not have to suffer my attempts at singing the Company song since there doesn't seem to be one. However, every morning a lot of the troops gather for their exercise/dance session to the most annoying music I have ever heard. So far I've resisted joining in, but I watch them with amusement from my office, although I think most of them just do it to waste a bit of time.

I look pretty dashing in my blue and khaki uniform made from some kind of sack-cloth. I have to wear a T-shirt under the shirt to stop my sensitive western skin getting rubbed raw. The trousers are so baggy that you could fit a few more people in (or perhaps I'm just small in that area?). The city of Liuzhou (you'll struggle to find it on a map) has 3 million people and some of the worst pollution I've ever seen, however it doesn't get very cold and today the sun is trying to shine through the haze. The language is virtually impossible and apart from the hellos and thank yous, every time I attempt something more adventurous such as "2 beers my good fellow and be jolly quick about it", they don't understand. The highlight in the morning is getting saluted by the factory guards as I sweep in through the gates with my driver. I've finally got some respect!!

I should be home for a few days over Christmas so give me a call.

Best wishes to you both.
Ma Ding

HAPPY DAYS – 7th January 2007

Well it's Sunday. Up at 6.30am and in to work. It was cold to start with but has now warmed up a bit with the sun coming through the haze. As I told you on the phone I bought you a special Liuzhou stone which I found in a strange stone market. It's not too big so I can bring it back in my suitcase next time. I bet you're very excited about getting a big pebble!!! I'm finding it much harder getting into the rhythm of the job again, maybe because I'm not feeling on top form at the moment. We've got the official opening on the 1st of February when all the VIPs from the local government, from GKN, key customers and suppliers, plus the British Consul General from Guangzhou will be here. So I've got a team of people preparing for the event. Also I've been asked to host a visit on Wednesday for some visitors from Sunderland City Council (Liuzhou is twinned with Sunderland); I'll probably have just as much problem with that language as I have with the Chinese.

I'm now getting pretty nifty with the chopstick things even though the hotel offers me a knife and fork from time to time. However I have one small problem ('only one?' I hear you say) which is difficult when we have large banquets. Being the only left handed user of chopsticks, not only do I get strange looks and nudge-nudge type comments from the natives, but when we have to sit tightly packed around a large circular table for a typical banquet I find that I'm constantly interfering with the right handed chopstick user on my left. As you know the Chinese educational system is quite strict and so everybody is taught at a very early age to use their right hand for just about everything, whilst in the UK we are a little more relaxed about these things. Anyway the result of all this is that I always get to have a conversation with the person sitting on my left about my left-handedness and then we usually find a way of taking it in turns to bring the chopsticks up and feed ourselves. Is this where the phrase 'elbow room' comes from? Obviously the person on my right hand side has extra space to eat with a flourish. The other day in order to prove that I could use these things effectively with the 'wrong' hand I was challenged to a peanut picking up contest. Luckily these were the soggy (soaked in brine?) type of peanuts and not the greasy, slippery peanuts we are used to, so I managed quite well much to the delight of the assembled diners.

January and February are really grotty months weather-wise even here in China.

Best wishes
Martyn

A typical picture stone formed naturally due to minerals seeping into the stone structure over millions of years.

HAPPY NEW YEAR – 8th January 2007

Happy New Year from deepest China. I travelled back to China on New Year's Day having lost my voice due to New Year's revelry. The cabin air on the planes for 16 hours made it worse so that when I arrived at work in China I sounded like a Mafiosi Godfather for three days. I took some of the world renowned Chinese medicine (some strange herb probably mixed with rat vomit) and the situation has steadily improved so that I'm now nearly normal!

Well the acquisition honeymoon period is now over so now I've got to start driving through business improvements. At the same time we're sorting out the factory buildings, putting in windows, filling holes in the floors and doing general cleaning. Updating the loos has gone to the bottom of the priority list and I'll probably run out of money before its turn comes around. Building relationships with customers and the local government/party officials is a key issue for getting things done, therefore I've got many evenings of eating half cooked chicken, live prawns and drinking the dreaded local fire water ahead of me!! We also need to get more power to run the new machines we're planning to buy; however, the local electricity monopoly wants more than £1.2 million to lay a new cable to the factory (more politics) . . .

It's not all work. The weekend before the Christmas break four of us travelled three and a half hours to one of the local tourist attractions near the city of Guilin. Spectacular scenery formed by natural acid rain over millions of years forming a strange mountain landscape with lakes and rivers. The weather was great and there was no pollution so you could even see the sky! I attach some pictures to give you an idea. We went rafting on bamboo rafts so we had to put plastic bags on our feet to keep dryish. If I hadn't had that weekend away I would definitely have felt very low.

The weather has now turned cold and windy here in Liuzhou. My language is improving slightly (I can now order more than one beer), the Bob the Builder uniform scratches less now that it's had a few washes and I've found a better place to buy really cheap DVDs.

Well it's head down for the next 39 days (and counting!) and I expect to be back home when the Chinese celebrate their New Year during the week 18th–24th February. After that I believe there'll be one more stretch until the end of April and then I'll take the summer off and get stuck in to all those jobs on Julie's lists (HELP!!!).

Best Wishes
Ma Ding

The latest footwear fashion in China!

The Karst landscape from the vantage point of a bamboo raft ride along the river near Guilin.

UPDATE FROM CHINA – 12th January 2007

(Message to AKR)

I bet you're thinking he only goes off to China when there is an impending disaster in our household, both the girls' cars broken at the same time. Thanks for helping out. Well following the New Year celebrations my sore throat just got worse during the flight out here, although a nice air steward (male) seemed a bit too concerned for my liking about me not being able to speak above a whisper. However a course of Chinese medicine (some herbs mixed with rat's vomit) seemed to do the trick and I'm now fighting fit, or as good as I'm ever going to be at my age! The Thursday after I got back we had a major power cut and had to close the factory for over a day, as a result we decided to take an early weekend (Friday and Saturday). It's now Friday the 12th and we started the week at 7.30am last Sunday so I'm really knackered. No visitors this weekend and I've decided not to work so I'll probably walk around a lot, getting stared at, maybe climb a local mountain but generally chill out.

We announced the new salary structure and management salaries this week, most of it based on their official earnings last year. However several managers came back and declared other non-payroll money that they were getting from various sources and therefore demanded additional increases. It's been a nightmare! I even had a conversation with one manager who told me that "it's OK to obtain money and not pay tax etc. as long as you don't get caught". And obviously I've had other people who are unhappy threaten to talk to the authorities if they don't get a pay rise. HELP!!

I've agreed to continue until the end of April and I believe they're interviewing people in Shanghai towards the end of the month. The City has agreed that people can let off fireworks this year so we have to arrange for extra covered storage for the hundreds of truck tyres we hold and also get more guards and fire extinguishers. I think your Chinese fire-fighting colleagues are going to have a fun week.

Best wishes from deepest China

MID WEEK BLUES – 17th January 2007

It's Wednesday and it's raining so a lot of the building work has come to halt. At least my office is warm. I'm having an apple and some monkey nuts for lunch because it's too cold and wet to walk to Greasy Zho's for some noodles. My hotel decided to upgrade itself to 5 star status last week and is now charging me an extra £2 per night. I wonder what they have to do to get upgraded? Either have a good lunch with the district hotel assessor or more probably just get a new notice printed and put it in the foyer. My negotiators have now agreed that I will get 2 little pieces of choccy by the bed each day, a bottle of wine in the room once a week and a 20% discount on the laundry. A glass of wine whilst I'm watching a film will be just like home!!! Since the upgrade we've lost power twice and had no hot water once; however, they have put a new carpet in the room and now supply bubble bath so I guess it all balances out. Yin and Yang as the Chinese say! I bought myself a new casual jacket for £12, it's a grey/blue thing, a bit different and goes with my blue troos and pully. (I'm even colour co-ordinated sometimes.) The watch strap of my ultra-expensive watch (Tim has the same one in gold only real, he claims) broke. I think it's going to be cheaper to buy a new watch and swap links over so I will have two that I can wear. These are the things that occupy my mind when I'm not at work, it's very sad!!!

My language is improving and I'm ordering food in the hotel restaurant in Chinese now (not by numbers!). The main problem is I only know the words for mushroom or fish soup and pork (obviously ice cream as well) so my menu is pretty limited. I think I'll find out the word for lamb tonight to make a change. Also, I am now sleeping a bit better although I wake up early and get to read my book in the bath for longer (always assuming there's hot water!).

We're supposed to have a team-building meeting this weekend so I'm trying to put together an agenda for that. The Sales Manager resigned today and the interim Financial

Controller finishes his contract in 3 weeks and doesn't want to extend it so we're having to find someone new in a very short time. Just the normal old work stuff!!!!

Only 30 days to go. Yeah!
Ma Ding

The Liuzhou Fandian, my home for the first session in China. My room was at the top left.

HOW ARE YOU? – 24th January 2007

(Message to RG)

I hear that Susan is now at home and progressing with her recovery. Please send her my very best wishes for a full and speedy return to normal. I'm not sure what the Chinese medicine would be for this type of problem. All I've discovered is that they have various potions made from herbs mixed with various animal body parts which together with acupuncture seem to be the cure for all ills. It certainly worked wonders for me with my recent sore throat.

Work is pretty tough and the language problem means that everything takes twice as long to understand and sort out. However things at the factory are progressing steadily and I think that we are slowly finding the right mix of GKN and Chinese culture. There is a lot of corruption in the business and as soon as we stopped some of the odd activities in the sales department the Sales Manager and two Account Managers left. We found out that they had been passing orders to the competition for several months, and the Sales Manager actually had some equity in one of the local competitors. So if you're looking for a fill-in sales job, brush up on your Chinese and come on over!

I'm really looking forward to coming home in 25 days' time (and counting). Although I now understand that BA staff are planning strikes during February so I'm obviously a bit concerned about the disruption. The weather's turned cold and wet here, much the same as the UK, so I probably wouldn't be playing golf anyway. I plan to take at least 4 months off after this assignment so I hope we can get some summer golf at your club.

Best wishes to you both
Ma Ding

HOW ARE YOU? – 25th January 2007

(Message to AKR)

Although it's been pretty wet and cold over the last couple of weeks I've managed to keep reasonably well. As I write this there's lots of banging and shouting as workers attempt to erect 3 large flag poles in preparation for our Official Opening next Thursday. The Mayor of Liuzhou and his entourage came to visit us yesterday (about 10 people, one of which was his official business card hander outer!) to talk about some of the problems we are having getting various acquisition documents finalised. He was OK, and understood most of my English, so with quite a lot of Chinese shouting, all the issues were sorted out. We've been trying to get the government departments to sort these things for the last 2 months without success, it just shows where the power and decision making lies.

Having actually eaten boiled pig's ear last weekend it'll be good to wash it down with a pint of beer with the same name (Pig's Ear Bitter) at the Woolpack in Slad! I can verify that the English beer of the same name has far more taste than the real thing although obviously not as chewy. I've just been informed by my Production Manager that there will be no electricity tomorrow (Friday) so we will have to change the weekend for the second time this year and start next Monday on Sunday (or something like that). I was really looking forward to a Sunday lie in this weekend.

My Chinese is slowly improving and I'm quite self-sufficient when ordering food and drink in the hotel now. Having said that my menu choice is pretty limited (by my language) and the waitresses always laugh, but they do just about understand with a bit of pointing as well. For example the word for soup is 'tang', but you have to say it flat, if you say it with a slight upward inflection it means sugar, and with a downward inflection it means hot. Luckily I have not yet received a bowl of sugar for my starter.

We tend to think we're pretty advanced in the west with our modern open plan offices and apartments. Well here in the factory we have open plan toilets, which is quite disconcerting. Well last week as part of our building improvement programme we put swing doors on the cubicles in the toilet block. No locks, but then you can look over the top to check if anyone's there. However, it seems that people now feel free to hide away and use electronic games and read newspapers etc. without being seen. Oh well, you win some, lose some.

The weather's turned warmish for the last couple of days which helps, although it gets cold by the evening. The air on Saturday was clear because the rain and wind had dispersed the pollution earlier in the week. It's starting to murk up a bit now though. I did lots of walking this weekend to pass the time. Ten miles on Saturday and about seven on Sunday, also some great views of the city from one of the local mountains. Actually these 'mountains' scattered around the city are reasonably high but do have steps built into the rock so it's fairly safe as long as you don't lose your footing. However I'm amazed how many local old codgers in their 60s and 70s can race up to the summit and once there proceed to strip down to their underwear and do Tai Chi type exercises. Not a pretty sight.

Well not much else to report. Just keeping my head down, counting the days and looking forward to a good long summer at home.

Best wishes
Martyn

View over Liuzhou city centre from one of the mountains close to the river.

FEBRUARY IN CHINA – 9th February 2007

What excitement, we had our Official Opening ceremony last week. The GKN 'Big Bosses' (and noses) flew in from the UK, the British Consul and his entourage flew up from Guangzhou (Canton) and lots of Big Wigs from the City turned up in big black cars. The local TV station also came along and interviewed my boss's boss! Lots of lion dances, rockets, raising of flags and unfortunately a series of boring speeches (including my introductory effort in Chinese which got a laugh). This was followed by tours of the factory and various meetings. The real highlight of the day was a Grand Banquet attended by about 100 people with some new dishes to try. On offer to tempt us all was boiled dog's willy and shark's swim bladder, mmm!! I did actually try the shark thing, very rubbery. In spite of the odd bits of food the evening degenerated due to the amount of drink consumed into a good old sing song, and we ended the evening joining hands in a big circle and singing Auld Lang Syne. The Chinese knew the tune but have their own words for this song so we took it in turns to sing alternate verses, one of ours and then one of theirs. We were all on an even footing (nothing to do with the drink) trying to understand the meaning of the song since even the best of the English-speaking Chinese couldn't understand the Rabbie Burns version and we didn't have a hope of making sense of the Chinese.

It's now the run-up period to the Chinese New Year and just like our Christmas there seem to be lots of parties going on. Last night I was invited to three banquets and ended up at the Foreign Affairs Bureau's bash for all the foreigners in Liuzhou. Unfortunately I had to give a short speech. Again the TV turned up to witness the spectacle. I managed to stay off the hard stuff so I'm feeling reasonably OK this morning. I can go for weeks without seeing any westerners in the City apart from the four guys who work at our factory. However last night about 30, a selection of Brits, Americans, Germans and Swedes came out of the woodwork. Most of the other

Brits are associated with the university and seem to be old men with young Asian wives!!! I've got three banquets to attend next week so I'm hoping to have a quiet weekend. Actually I've got no choice since there are no visitors staying over.

The weather has remained warmish for the last week but without wind the pollution has got worse. I'm really getting used to the strange sights. For lunch, 2 or 3 days a week we walk down the road to 'Greasy Zho's' to have some rice thing with bits of stuff on top and usually we pass someone selling several cooked dogs, snakes and dried fish. This morning driving into work we were overtaken by someone on a motorbike carrying 3 dead pig carcasses on the back of the bike and their heads (I am assuming they were once attached) were tied on to the crash bars. I must get my camera out again.

I eventually signed my contract extension to take me until the end of April. Anyway, only 8 days to go until I get back home for a week. I'm really looking forward to it although I understand it's a bit chilly at the moment.

Best wishes to you all,
Ma Ding

My management team (in blue and beige) with several VIPs for the official opening.

Food options for sale outside the factory. Luvvly!!

21

WHAT'S MA DING DONE? – 8th March 2007

Well I'm now back in China after a wet, but relaxing week at home. I seem to have brought the rain back with me because it's been cold and wet for the last week and a bit. When it's not raining hard there's a steady drizzle that just floats around and gets everywhere! I'm told that in a couple of weeks' time when the Feng Zhu tree blossoms the weather will turn good for the summer, so I hope it's good for Julie's visit in early April. The dodgy weather did not stop the on-going Lunar New Year celebrations everywhere in the city, lots of red banners, lanterns and fireworks. In fact the last day of the festival (the equivalent of our Twelfth Night) the whole city was ablaze with fireworks from 8.00pm until past 11.00pm, and I just stayed in my hotel room (10th floor) by the open window and watched the panoramic display, including a couple of rockets which missed my window by only a few feet.

The wife of one of our ex-pats, who helped teach English to some of our employees, left to go back to the UK to resume her job with the BBC after a 9 month break. We held an English party for her Chinese students (about 25) by giving them a typical English day's food and some English party games. So, cornflakes and Tetley's tea for breakfast, egg sandwiches and warm beer for lunch, and shepherd's pie for supper, interspersed with Jaffa Cakes, sherry, pork scratchings and the one thing the Chinese really struggled to eat, Barratt's Liquorice Allsorts! Games included: pin the tail on the donkey, pass the parcel and a pub quiz. All good fun and I, as ever, had to give out the prizes.

We're still not making a profit but we are just ahead of budget so it's not too bad. Unfortunately with all our focus on health and safety one lady press operator, who'd been working for 8 days in a row and had just returned from her lunch break, lost concentration and chopped off the tops of 3 fingers, one of which was sewn back on. So all hell has broken out from the Group HQ and we're doing major risk assessment reviews of all equipment. We'll probably end up guarding everything and having to get new equipment and more people to maintain production output. The HR manager resigned last week, mainly due to the fact that his family home is 3 hours away and he's got fed up travelling; he also thought he would get a huge pay rise from the new owners, but that didn't happen. So I'm now doing all the HR stuff as well.

I bought my 3rd copy of the new James Bond DVD this week. The first was an awful copy with the projector noise overriding the soundtrack, the second was in Russian with a mixture of English and Chinese subtitles, anyway this copy seems OK. I'll have spent £1.30 on 3 DVDs just to get one that works!!

Not much else to report really, I'm eating all the odd stuff regularly now and I haven't been ill once since I've been in China (tempting fate a bit!).

Best wishes,
Ma Ding
PS: the word for 'understand' is 'dong', so 'Martyn understands' translates as 'Ma Ding dong'. Didn't Chuck Berry have a song like that?

COUNTDOWN!!! – 23rd March 2007

I've now got 2 clocks running. The first, it's only 10 days until Julie gets here, and the second, 38 days until it's all over. I need to make the best use of the time but I also really want to get home.

This week has been very changeable, on Monday the humidity was so high everything was wet, including paperwork in the office, and all our steel and unpainted wheels have gone rusty. The painting process couldn't get the paint to stick to the metal, all the floors and walls were dripping with condensation. Tuesday was just a wet rainy day and then Wednesday turned out to be pleasant and sunny, Thursday cold and dry and today is just like a drizzly, overcast, grey day in the UK.

I had a good trip last weekend to a place called Chengdu about an hour's flight from here. I went to see the giant pandas at the Research and Breeding Centre, see some museums, ancient irrigation works and climb a mountain. The weather was great on the Saturday and there were about 30 pandas wandering about this place which has tried to replicate their natural habitat. I attach a piccy of me and my new panda friends. The Sunday was colder but I climbed up this mountain into the clouds and mist. Couldn't see a thing from the top, a 2 hour climb to the summit 1260 metres above sea level. It's the centre for the Daoist religion so there were lots of temples embedded into the side of the mountain and in typical Chinese fashion people were selling water and cucumbers at every opportunity. I only saw one other westerner the whole weekend so lots of people were staring at me. I was looked after by one of our suppliers, and a young chap called Brian Li, who lives in Chengdu and is a friend of my assistant Karen, acted as my personal translator. After all the climbing my legs were a bit dodgy on the Monday!!

I'm slowly getting better at the language which is just as well because this weekend there are no visitors, I'm staying in Liuzhou so I will be fending for myself and I can't stand eating in the hotel restaurant all weekend.

I did get to learn Mah Jong last Wednesday as I joined a

few folks from work. Mah Jong is a cross between dominoes, rummy and bridge. To add to the excitement we played for chocolate. I'm sure they let me win a few times because I'm the boss, but it was good fun and I'll try to play one evening next week and get better. Other than that evenings are mostly eat, bath, read and watch a DVD (in various languages).

We had another accident in the factory this week; a piece of metal fell over and broke someone's foot. Luckily he was wearing safety shoes or it would have been a lot worse. The lady who lost her fingers is still in hospital nearly 3 weeks later. A worker in the UK also lost a finger at about the same time and he was discharged from the NHS hospital after 3 days. I now understand what's going on. Here in China the works accident is covered by insurance so the hospital can continue to claim money all the time someone remains with them, it's a great form of income. So the guy with the broken metatarsal will probably stay in hospital until 2009!! We are the first company in the city to train First Aiders. The Red Cross from Guangxi Province have been with us this week training 22 of our employees and yesterday the local press and TV crew turned up to interview me on why we are doing this training. Isn't it obvious? We're getting quite a lot of good publicity in the city.

I've decide to take the company cars away from the senior managers from the 1st April. These were cars given to the company at various times instead of the customer paying for the wheels in cash. Yet another way that the previous bosses could get a personal gain from the business. Most of the cars are costing a fortune in repairs and servicing so we are getting rid of 13 and keeping the best 3 (one for me and my driver!!!).

A GKN main board director is visiting us next week with the boss of GKN China. I like the fact that I am in a unique position to tell the truth about the issues here, the support (or lack of) from the centre on several things, odd decisions being made for us without understanding local conditions etc.
Great fun not having to worry about internal politics.

Zaijian (goodbye), Ma ding dong bang mang
(bangmang = help)

White face and big nose, which one is the panda?

TOP-HEAVY!!! – 28th March 2007

I was recently travelling from Liuzhou to Guilin airport on what must be one of the worst motorways in China, potholes and repairs everywhere on a two-lane road. Heavy trucks, coaches and cars weave about constantly at various speeds trying to avoid the hazards. This in turn leads to many crashes which only makes the problems worse. Anyway, on this trip we were held up trying to get past a large truck which had toppled over on a bend and its load of tomatoes had spread everywhere. Not only that but several local peasants and some wild dogs (wolves?) had decided that here was an opportunity too good to pass up and were salvaging/eating as much as they could regardless of the danger posed by motorway traffic. The truck probably hadn't been travelling particularly fast but was, as I had seen on many occasions, overloaded and completely top-heavy.

This got me thinking that many things in China are top-heavy, not just vehicles, large and small, carrying enormous loads. The structure of the state-owned business that we acquired in Liuzhou had several layers of management; General Manager, Deputy GM, Senior Managers, Assistant Senior Managers, Middle Managers, Junior Managers, Supervisors, Shift Foremen and Charge hands. Certainly top-heavy!! It's interesting that the Chinese Pavilion currently being constructed in Shanghai as the centre-piece for the World Expo also reflects this top-heavy theme. As a business we supply more than one million wheels a year to one of our biggest customers; a General Motors joint venture based in Liuzhou making small vans. Now in Europe we have car transporters that may carry up to seven vehicles at a time, 4 on top and 3 below. Well the transporters for these vans eclipse this by a long way and provide yet another example of the Chinese 'top-heavy' capability. Seven vans on the lower level and sixteen (yes, sixteen!), two rows of eight, on the top, a grand total of 23 vans. Although I've seen many of these transporters over my time in China, I'm amazed that I've yet to see one topple over … yet!!!

23 vans on one transporter.

The Chinese centre-piece for the 2010 Expo in Shanghai.

Shop signs are a constant source of amusement and I've often thought that there would be a good job for someone just correcting some of these howlers. However, I'm sure that if we attempted to put up Chinese signs in the UK we would make just as many errors. Analysing this further during one of my bored moments I decided I could classify these signs into three main categories. Firstly, a direct translation of the Chinese sign, secondly, western words chosen to reflect what the owners think the shop activity should be and thirdly what seems to be a random selection of letters which may or may not be pronounceable. Another thing I've noticed with this effort the Chinese are making is that they're trying to ensure their shop fronts give an air of western chic. As with many long-established western businesses there is often a smaller notice stating something like: 'Est. 1876' or 'Since 1898'. Well I've seen several with signs saying 'Since 2006' which given that it's only just 2007 makes a bit of a mockery of trying to give the customer confidence that the business has traded successfully for a long time. Having said that, the rate of opening and closure of Chinese high street businesses is amazing. Many a time I've gone back to buy something I saw a few weeks previously only to find the original shop closed and something completely different in its place, such is the pace of change in China. They should probably put the new westernised shop sign up with the addition of 'Since last Thursday'!

Examples of my new theory are shown below:

Best Wishes

A direct translation of the Chinese characters.

An English sounding word that may or may not attract the customers.

Some western letters that could just about be pronounced.

WAITING … – 3rd April 2007

I'm sitting in a modern airport somewhere in the middle of China near a place called Zhengzhou. I can't check in yet because nothing appears to be open. Also because there was a problem with the 6.30am transport from the factory I was visiting 2 hours' drive away, I'm here on my own, the only western face. I'm now on my way to meet up with Julie this evening in Hong Kong; if my 2 flights and her long haul are roughly on time we should meet in the baggage hall. (I'm not too optimistic the timing will work out.) So I've been here at a meeting of the GKN General Managers of China, plus some head office hangers on. The hotel was one of the worst I've ever stayed in; grey towels, no hot water and very grubby; still it was only £50 for 3 nights including breakfast. (I hope Julie's expectations are not too high for her hotels this week.) Apart from the meeting itself we spent 2 hours travelling by coach to visit the famous 'local' attraction which was the Shaolin Temple. This is the main centre for Kung Fu, that martial art going back thousands of years. So apart from seeing several monks and some Kung Fu trainees, I did buy a book so that I can practise during my summer break. Beware!

I'm feeling a little jaded this morning. The business here is a joint venture and the boss of the partner is the head honcho in town and so decided to try to drink us under the table with this horrible baijiu firewater stuff. Then we ended up at some Karaoke bar where we were forced to sing. The local GKN boss, Phil and I did an average rendition of Return to Sender by Elvis. Well we thought it was average and the Chinese seemed to like it since they applauded. Thinking about it later they probably applauded as we were getting off the stage and not doing another song.

Only 28 days to go until my contract ends, hurrah. Hopefully the week touring around some parts of China will make time go quickly. The check-in now appears to be manned so I'll see if they'll accept my ticket and passport and get me started on the journey home.

Best wishes
Ma Ding

You don't really want to hear this but I'll give it 9 out of 10 for commitment.

COUNTDOWN RESET – 13th April 2007

Well, Julie spent last week with me in China. We visited various places including Hong Kong, the Terry Cotta warriors in Xi'an, the strange mountain scenery near here and finally the city of Liuzhou (including the obvious highlight, a factory visit!!). Apart from the usual problems of toilets and strange food it all went very well. Many of my work colleagues asked why I married someone so young. I think what they meant was why Julie married an old fart like me. My reply is that it's the hard work that I do that has aged me, whilst Julie benefits from me living away from home so much.

The arrangements for my replacement have slipped a few weeks so I've tried to accommodate the situation by staying here until the 25th May. It was easy to say at the time and Julie's already spent the extra money, but now I'm thinking should I have just stuck to the original plan to get back on the 1st May. On the other hand I probably want to keep the door open for another assignment some time. The weather's getting stickier and it's definitely becoming more polluted, which you can even taste on bad days. I got measured up for my Bob the Builder summer uniform yesterday, so if it arrives on time (before I depart) I'll become this year's fashion icon in Liuzhou. They don't seem to worry about the inside leg measurement, therefore I expect the trousers to have a low slung crotch. Or it could be that the lady measuring me decided it was bad form to get too much detail from a 'big nose'. The business is slowly improving and although we are not yet making a profit we are ahead of forecast and budget for the year so far which means the big bosses in England do not push me too hard. I've just got to get April right and then I can leave with my reputation intact (as what I'm not sure!). Lots of visitors in the next 2 weeks so I hope it makes the time go a little quicker and there will be people to have dinner with in the evenings.

I played Mah Jong for the second time last night (it's a mixture of dominoes and rummy with lots of shouting), and this time for money, and ended up winning 12RMB, about

75p. Still it all helps! Although I've now been told that the local rule is that the winner has to buy drinks for the playing partners so I'll be out of pocket on the activity. But it was good fun for a couple of hours. I start proper Chinese language lessons next Thursday, much too late, but there's a group of 4 of us and we need to be seen to make the effort since about 80 Chinese employees are learning English. I think I mentioned in one of my previous e-mails that we were selling off the company cars. We had them valued and yesterday we put up a notice with the list of 13 cars (2 are actually illegal) with an expected price and within an hour they had all been sold. We actually made a profit on the deal, more than we've made in the real business!!! Perhaps a fundamental change of business strategy is called for?

I hope you are all well and looking forward to summer; I am.

Best Wishes
Martyn

Playing Ma Jiang for chocolate.

EXTRA TIME – 1st May 2007

Dajia hao (hello everybody),

Today is May 1st, the start of the Chinese May Golden Week Holiday. 7 days' holiday for most employees across China. Not me, I'm in the office with a few of the finance staff sorting out the April month end numbers and other reporting requirements for GKN. I hope we can have this finished by Thursday midday and then I can take a few days off. I borrowed a bike from one of the Brits who's gone back to the UK this week so today I thought I'd try to cycle in to work from the hotel, hoping that the traffic would be light due to the holiday. It normally takes about 25 minutes by car in heavyish traffic so I thought it might take about 40 minutes or so. I left the hotel at 8.00am and after 15 minutes realised I'd forgotten my office key. With no one else in to open the door I had no option but to cycle back to get my key. Off I set again but this time I got a bit lost in an area of little shops and winding roads under a major overpass intersection (bikes are not allowed on this overpass). By the time I managed to find the correct route the sun was high in the sky, so when I finally got to the factory at 9.15am I was dripping. I took my shirt off to dry it in front of the air-con unit and had just sat down topless when Mr Wong, my Finance Manager walked in. For all he knew I could have been totally naked. Not a pretty sight! (for him) I'm not sure he believed my explanation so I don't know what new reputation I'll have got now. They'll probably think it's some strange western custom to go topless on the first of each month.

Only 25 days to go. My leaving announcement has been prepared and I will talk to everyone next week. I'm sure it'll be a shock particularly as there isn't a permanent replacement available yet. I will have done 7 months which is more than enough.

The last few days has been solid rain but yesterday evening it all cleared up and today is expected to be about 30 degrees C. The outlook is for this to continue for the rest of the week. The City is hosting an 'International Clown Festival' in one of the parks all this week so I'm planning to go along on Friday or Saturday. As ever I expect I'll be the only westerner or big nose. The locals might even mistake me for one of the clowns. I think I'll take my juggling balls along and earn a few kuai (local money).

I'm really fed up with eating in the hotel and the things on the menu that are worth eating are just boring me. It's very difficult to eat out on my own because although I know lots of words for food things I can't read a menu. Also people don't eat in Chinese restaurants on their own. The result of all this is that over the last few weeks I've lost over a stone (7kg). Most of it from my gut, but a few other parts are definitely looking smaller!!! I do feel better for it and will need to buy some new clothes in the next few weeks. The trick will be not putting it back on again when I get back to Julie's (never been known to under-cater) cooking.

I'll continue to take the weekly Chinese language lessons up until I leave as you never know when it'll come in handy. The Chinese are definitely taking over the world.

I hope you are all enjoying the early summer.

Best Wishes

My office with the famous air-con unit in the corner used for drying sweaty shirts!!!

FAILED PICTURE SEND – 19th May 2007

I tried sending the e-mail below on Friday, but it got thrown back because the picture size was too big. So here is yesterday's e-mail without the piccies (you'll have to imagine it), and I'll be home this time next week.

Obviously I'm still counting down, thinking this time next week I'll have checked out for the final time from the hotel etc. The Finance Manager, Mr Wei has just been to see me and told me how sorry he is to see me leave and that he really enjoyed my management style. It's going to be difficult over the next few days.

A small group of us took a trip to visit a famous waterfall on the China, Vietnam border last weekend. The De Tian Falls are the second largest cross-border waterfalls in the world, the largest being the Niagara Falls between the USA and Canada. Recently the e-mail speed has been a bit variable so it's been difficult to send or receive pictures, but I'll try. The water was pretty low as it's not yet the rainy season, so the waterfall was not as impressive as I hoped, but the area was very beautiful and not yet very touristy. The other picture is of me inside the Vietnamese border with the border stone marking the entrance into China. There was a border guard just out of the picture but he was quite happy for us to wander into Vietnam for a few minutes.

It's raining quite hard here today, but it's needed because the air has been getting more polluted every day this week. Hopefully the rain will clear the air for the weekend.

Best wishes to all
Ma Ding

De Tian waterfall on the China–Vietnam border.

Standing by the Vietnam border marker.

THE MIDDLE KINGDOM – 21st May 2007

(Final Message)

Well, it's now only 5 days to go before I say goodbye to China and I've got a party with different groups of people every night. I'll need to go home for a rest just because of the leaving parties! I'm full of mixed emotions; on the one hand I really want to get back to family and friends and my normal life, on the other side I'm leaving something that's unfinished and not handing over to a permanent successor. I want to get back to home cooking, some clean air and even a game of golf. It'll be good to get out of the hotel room I've been living in like some reclusive film star for the last seven months. I will obviously miss many of the Chinese people that have supported me and helped me during my time in China, most of them have a great sense of humour (well you've got to laugh if pig's willy and fish bladder is part of your everyday food). Many of them are asking when I'll be back, it's very difficult.

I did a lot of walking this weekend, everyone had gone home so I was on my own. So tonight I'll go and have a foot massage (honest), I've had it done once before. It costs £2.50 for 45 minutes and they do spend most of the time washing and kneading the feet, on occasion they find the pressure point that makes my ears go fizzy (somehow it's all connected) and for some reason they finish the foot massage at about mid-thigh level. Don't worry, I keep my loose fitting trousers on all the time!

The summer uniforms arrived today and it has to be said they look just as bad as the winter uniforms, just lighter cloth and short sleeves. I still look crap wearing it. We've got a few visitors this week, which is just as well since I've accumulated various things over my time here and don't have enough room in my suitcase to get it all back, as it is I'll be above the weight limit. The company got a prize from the City government today, a large wooden and brass plaque with red and black Chinese writing on it. I've been told it is a prize to 'encourage' us to make profits and pay more tax, and we even got a brown envelope given to us with about £1,000 in. Previously, I am told, this money would probably have disappeared into the finance department manager's pockets, however this time 'honest Mart' has put it back into our current account.

I'm sure I'll get back to China sometime to see all the things that I didn't get the time to visit. All in all a very interesting experience but I'll be glad to be back home.

I look forward to seeing you over the summer.

Best Wishes
Zaijian (goodbye)
Ma Ding (Martyn)

Pig's face from the nostril end!! It tasted better than it looked (honest!).

The Second Session
Becoming Familiar

Back to the same factory in Liuzhou where the General Manager who replaced me after my first session decided he had to return to the UK for family reasons. However the factory had improved and the main task for this assignment was to ensure sales and profit growth.

E-mails, April to September 2008

TO CHINA AGAIN!! – 7th April 2008

I am now waiting for the driver to pick me up and take me to Heathrow. Yes, Terminal 5, so I might not be going anywhere and if I do, the suitcase with my 3 months' worth of supplies might not go in the same direction!

Since I returned to the UK last summer GKN has failed to get a new Chinese General Manager for the business in Liuzhou. The Chinese managers who are any good just don't want to work/live in this city. The guy who took over from me has had enough so I got the call a few days ago. GKN have had a lot of senior management changes over the last few months so this gives me the opportunity to get back in. The other jobs I was pursuing in France, South Africa and the UK were just taking ages to come to a conclusion (one way or the other) as everyone seems very cautious about the world economy. So a bird in the hand is worth . . . and my Chinese language training will now come in handy as I am now able to say . . . "No, I don't want to eat boiled dog's willy".

I'll let you know my e-mail address when I get there.

Best regards
Martyn

DEJA VU ... or HUI KAN (Chinese) – 22nd April 2008

Well, I'm back again in the Chinese hot seat. And it is hot, the weather has been very humid the last few days with temperatures reaching over 30 degrees. The factory is still a bit of a building site as phase two of the building upgrades and equipment layout is well underway. There has been a lot of superficial improvement since I was last here but some of the basic problems still exist. The improved output has mostly been achieved with extra overtime. It all feels very familiar and it was very easy to get back into the swing of things again. This time however there is only one other natural English speaker out here, all the other ex-pats decided to go home after their stint and no others were available to replace them. I also think that there is a cost issue in putting more ex-pats out here, but it does feel a bit light on GKN experts.

I also have the same room back at the hotel ('that strange English big nose is back') and the toaster in this supposedly 5 star hotel still doesn't work, so noodles for breakfast again!!! The city is still being reconstructed with a huge underpass and underground shopping area being built which has totally screwed up the traffic flow. There seems to be much more traffic about anyway so getting to work and back is slower although some of the strange driving activities make for lots of amusement. A lot of change in the few months I've been away.

My newfound Chinese language skills have come in handy both at work, in the hotel restaurant and around town. I tried to buy a small suitcase at the weekend and ended up with a crowd of about 15 shop staff and others witnessing my negotiating skills in Chinese, Everybody had a good laugh, including me. And I managed to get 2 pounds off the price!! I'm due to start Chinese lessons tonight with one other person who I think is much further on than me so I'll have to work hard to catch up.

I've decided not to stay in this city and just walk around every weekend. This time I'm going to visit other places now that I have more confidence with the language. I plan to go to Canton (now called Guangzhou) this weekend which is about an hour away by plane. It's a city with lots of history and there is a trade fair on at the moment so one of the sales guys will be around on the Saturday. My visa is only valid for one 30 day entry so I must sort that out next week or I'll be coming back home soon. The visa process has been toughened up a bit with the Olympics security concerns.

I hope you are all keeping well. Please let me know what fun things I am missing back in cold England.

Best wishes
Huo Ma Ding

My room at the Liuzhou Fandian. My home from home all through the first session and back again for the second session.

NEARLY HOME (for a week) – 9th May 2008

Dear All,

It's Friday, the end of a 6 day working week. Yesterday was so hot, 31 degrees, I put the air-conditioning system on. Today however we had torrential rain for most of the late morning until mid-afternoon. A few of us went out for lunch and saw several scooters lying on their sides in the middle of roads. Aqua-planing on an electric scooter is not fun. I was persuaded to go to the newly opened Pizza Hut for lunch. It was OK, the quality was quite good but it was at UK prices (£7 for a pizza). At the moment it is very full as all of the Chinese youths think anything western/American is wonderful. They'll change their minds when they are fat and broke!!!

My passport with an annual work visa arrived back late yesterday, which was just as well because yesterday was my last day allowed in China (30 limit) so today I would have had to either go to Hong Kong and try to get a new visa or just be an illegal alien for a while. All the visitors have gone back so I'm literally the only natural English speaker here at the moment. I'm on my own this weekend so I'll do the normal thing of walk around, a bit of shopping, watch a DVD and sleep a lot. I've seen all the films on the hotel system, in fact they have only added 3 new films from when I was here last year, so I have to buy films at 70p each, it's tough!!! The hotel has now opened the swimming pool which is advertised as having a 'conntrolled tenperatur' for 'our distingushd guests'. I tried it last weekend and it is pretty big; 50 by 40 metres, and a good temperature, also no-one else seems to use it

My assistant Karen got married to a German chap last week (Werner Hermann) and she will leave at the end of June to spend 3 months in Germany. I'm not sure if she'll come back, but in any case I will need to get a replacement who understands my strange ways with the English language! My Chinese teacher, Matata, is interested but I'm not sure if she would be tough enough when I get annoyed with people (which I do occasionally). We had a test at the Chinese lesson last Tuesday and I came 2nd (only 2 in the class though). And for this week's homework we have to learn a Chinese song called 'Ming Ming Bai Bai'. I'm not sure what it all means but it does have a catchy tune and people look at me in a strange way when I walk around the factory and the city singing it out of tune.

Last Tuesday morning my Production Manager Mr Meng came to see me and explained that one of his key workers had unfortunately been killed in a car crash. I obviously asked him to express my condolences to his wife who also works at our factory and asked him what we would normally do in these circumstances. It seems that the company would usually pay 80% of the funeral costs and provide other help as necessary. I gave my permission to continue this practice. Well, on the Thursday Mr Meng came to see me again but this time he seemed a bit sheepish. "Martyn," he said, "you know the guy who died on Tuesday. Well he turned up for work today." I was obviously taken aback but this is China and I've got used to surprises, however this was a new one on me. It seemed that this chap had run up some gambling debts and decided that faking his death might be a good way out, so he asked his wife to tell the company he had died. However the whole exercise had become a bit too complicated to handle so he decided to come back to work expecting to continue as if nothing had happened. Without going into all the details of the disciplinary process we eventually fired him and gave his wife a written warning even after the local Bureau of Employment tried to defend his actions. Even after nearly 30 years of working I'm still experiencing new situations. It's interesting!

Only 3 weeks to go and I'll get home for a long week because the Chinese have a national holiday (dead snakes' day or something) on Monday 9th June. Next weekend I have a customer meeting on Saturday in Shanghai so I'll meet up with some old colleagues for dinner on the Saturday and maybe do a museum or something on the Sunday before flying back in the evening. I'm now nearly mid-way through my contract but there is no sign of a Chinese General Manager on the horizon so unless something happens in the next couple of weeks I'll probably sign up for another 2 months.

I hope the British summer has kicked in now.

Best wishes
Martyn

LATEST NEWS – 16th May 2008

I understand that the Chinese earthquake is getting regular TV coverage outside China and it is constantly being updated here on several channels. It really is a tragedy and the numbers of dead will only get worse. The government is currently accepting that up to 50,000 might be the outcome but as so many outlying towns have yet to be reached no-one can be sure. I received several e-mails asking if I was OK, others asking if the 'earth had moved for me' (not for a long time). So, just so you know, there was some shaking in parts of our city although I personally didn't feel anything. Some cities further away than us from the epicentre had damage and obviously Chengdu and the closer areas have been very badly affected. We are all getting involved in the rescue effort and will be donating money and giving blood next week. Several of my employees have family in the affected area and had difficulty getting information but so far we understand that none of their relatives have been killed. It's a tragedy that so many school children have died, which as a result of the single child policy will mean parents losing their families and a whole generation being lost from many towns. *(Note: the final official death toll was 70,000 with nearly 20,000 missing.)*

Due to the summer heat we are now having a two hour lunch break at the factory. It's OK for those who can go home, cook a meal and have a nap, but for me all it means is a longer working day for the same pay!! Now I know why some of the senior managers have sofas in their offices, they close the door and have a good sleep.

Well on Wednesday night I was having a wonderful dream where someone was stroking my hair and face. As I felt my cheek being tapped I woke up to find this huge insect on my face, I knocked it onto the pillow and captured it in a glass. It was a huge cockroach thing with a body about 4cm long and antennae of a similar length. I then tried to get back to sleep without success wondering whether cockroaches travel in pairs. In the morning I presented the insect to the manager of this 5 star hotel and half expected him to tell me it was all part of the in-room catering service! I then went for breakfast and had my daily battle to get a decent slice of toast. By the time I'd got to the factory the hotel had rung my assistant to express their deep regrets etc. When I returned to the hotel in the evening most of the staff were aware of the problem and a letter of apology together with a platter of fruit was in my room. I'm told they will probably give me a bottle of wine at the weekend as a goodwill gesture. I will wait and see.

We have tried out a few assistants/translators this week to replace Karen who is off to Germany for 3 months. Matata, my Chinese teacher was OK, then there was a girl named Doe who just couldn't understand me at all and yesterday there was someone called Jane who also struggled but said that she was very nervous. Next Tuesday Celina (whoever she is) is going to try. I really don't hold out too much hope. I'm now able to hold the odd (very odd) meeting in Chinese and usually get my message across and it's OK for simple things. However, as General Manager I'm often trying to communicate motivational or conceptual issues (I bet some of you didn't think I knew those words) and I do need someone who can communicate what I mean and not just translate the words.

I'm looking forward to getting back home for a few days at the end of the month. Hopefully I'll get to see some of you and catch up on the exciting UK news.

Best Wishes from the East.
Ma Ding

BACK IN ZHONG GUO (China) – 14th June 2008

Well I've been back in China nearly one week and it's been very busy. I go for several weeks without a visitor and then just like buses they all come at once. My boss, his Finance Director and the divisional IT Director were here most of the week and we also had three sets of customers, two of which were doing internal audits. All of the above were requiring my presence, not just during the normal working day, but also during lunch and in the evenings. However it did make the week go quickly!

Wednesday, Thursday and Friday saw pissistent heavy rain, so much so that on Friday many of the roads were flooded and it took over an hour to drive the 4 miles to the factory. My boss who was due to fly out on Friday morning couldn't get to the local airport because of floods (the airport was also closed) so we rearranged for him to be taken to Guilin (4 hours in the car due to the flooding) so that he could fly home sometime. I really didn't want him hanging around any longer!! The highlight of the week was Thursday evening when I had no choice but to take my boss, Brian, and a French visitor, Phillipe, out for dinner. They both wanted a real Chinese meal but we couldn't invite anyone else because of the confidential nature of our discussions. So for the first time, without any help whatsoever I had to order a meal (and it had to be good!!!) in Chinese. Apart from the fact that most of the waitresses came over to the table to see this 'big nose' attempt to order soup (mushroom), beer and wine, and various dishes it all turned out fine with lots of laughter. The only dish that seemed a bit odd was a pork dish that was just very sweet fat rather than meat. It was also a bit of a language challenge because the French guy had limited English so my linguistic skills were stretched during the evening. Obviously I then asked for a pay increase! (The boss will think about it!)

Today is very hot (about 33 degrees) and humid. I thought about buying a pair of casual trousers but by the time I've walked to the shops I'm very sweaty so it's probably not good to try on new clothes etc.; after half an hour it's time to come back for a shower. I'll try later this evening when it will be a bit cooler I hope. I'm told that it'll only get hotter in July.

The European cup football is on Chinese TV most evenings but it is at least 2 days behind and it's a challenge to see who is playing because all the writing is in Chinese, so unless I know who some of the players are it's very difficult. Anyway it will give me something to watch over the next few days apart from DVDs and BBC World (which only works when it is not raining, probably because the satellite gets full of water).

I hope you are all well and enjoying the summer sunshine!!

Best wishes
Ma Ding

BUYING TROUSERS (the sequel) – 16th June 2008

Further to my previous e-mail, you might recall that I was waiting until it was cooler (and I was less sweaty) before going to buy some trousers. Anyway there was much fun with me trying to find the right colour and style. The Chinese shop assistants have a habit of bringing everything out for you, even though you've made it clearish what you are looking for. I managed to tell them that I wanted a pleated front and a particular colour. Then came the fun of the size. Well the trousers are marked up as 30, 31, 32, etc. which I assumed to be the waist measurement. I was right, but the number refers to a Chinese 'inch' equivalent which is about 20% bigger than our inch. So me thinking I'm a 33 waist means that in China I'm a 27 (this should be good news for many of you!!!!). Also I was anticipating an inside leg measurement from the pretty young female assistant, only to find that they do the outside leg only and I'm a 31, the same as my English inside leg. Confused?? I tried them on and they fitted well apart from the length. Three inches too long!! (I know I'm a short a***!) So I said they were too long and was told "no problem, by the time you have paid for them they will be altered".

Now the Chinese department store method of paying is very complicated, the assistant writes out 3 pieces of paper, then you have to find the payment counter, pay the money, get various stamps and other glued bits on more forms and then you return to the original sales counter. By the time I'd done all that (about 8 minutes) my trousers had been professionally altered and put in a classy carton. That is service for you! I'll try it at M&S next time and see what response I get.

It rained all day Sunday and is still raining now late Monday afternoon. Lots of flooding in the area and 55 people have drowned in our province and Guangdong, the province to the east.

Best wishes
Martyn with smart new troos!

My local laundry (laungry) facility.

UPDATE FROM CHINA – 30th June 2008

It's never boring here!! You may have seen on the news that Southern China has had some tropical storms over the last week or so. Lightning and lashing rain like I've never seen before. In fact I was standing on the balcony outside my office watching the storm when a bolt of lightning struck a long metal ladder on the building opposite, about 50m away. The flash of light and loud crack was very frightening. Luckily no one was hurt and I spent the rest of the day inside. The next day our workshops were flooded and all electrical equipment was stopped. It was also incredibly difficult to get back to the hotel with vehicles abandoned everywhere and others avoiding the flooded roads. Now it's turned very hot and humid, about 36 degrees so we are having to provide drinks and extra rest periods for the work force.

The factory is next to a school and so this week we cannot use the large production presses during the day as the students have exams all week, also we keep getting complaints about using this equipment at night because it disturbs other neighbours. So it's all a bit difficult!! And yet the Chinese are so noisy when it suits them!!

On Friday I came down to breakfast expecting to have the same toast availability problem (please see previous e-mails) only to see a large metal cage next to the toaster containing a 5ft alligator. I've heard of 'snap' (crackle and pop) for breakfast but this is ridiculous. Luckily its jaws were taped closed and it seemed pretty quiet so I just had my normal toast (through the toaster 4 times to get some colour) and fruit. On Saturday the alligator was still there but on Sunday only an empty cage. I guess the Saturday evening banquet/wedding reception must have consumed the creature, and as this is China probably used the leftovers for a pair of shoes and a belt for the happy couple!!!

I've just come back from the District government offices where they were presenting 'encouragement money' to some of the local companies. I was the only western face amongst about 500 people so the TV cameras kept panning round to include me. I had to go up to the podium and collect a big wooden and brass plaque and 10,000 RMB in used notes (about £1,500). It all comes in handy when you're trying to make the half year results!!! We also seem to have got an award of 300,000 RMB from the Bureau of Science and Innovation for something. It's all about who you have lunch with. I will need to host a banquet to say thank you in the next few weeks when we get the cash!! I hope they don't want to eat alligator!

I'm off to GKN HQ in Shanghai next week. Very plush offices with no expense spared, a far cry from the real dirty factories around China. Well it will make a change of scenery and probably won't be as humid.

I broke my reading glasses the other day and so had great fun trying to buy a new pair. Again it was a case of all the assistants in the optician's coming to stare and laugh at me trying to explain what I wanted, at first they thought I expected a repair, then they tried to fix me up with Nana Mouskouri type glasses. In the end I settled for a pair that double fold so I can easily lose them! My Chinese is slowly improving and I can hold short meetings at work as long as the subject isn't too technical.

You will recall that my Chinese name is Huo Ma Ding and most people refer to me (to my face that is) as Ma Ding. However I've noticed that some of the Chinese now call me Lao Ma which means Old Horse. Now this isn't as bad as it sounds since the Chinese respect older people and so to call someone 'Lao' is a term of deference. In fact in the Quality department both the director and one of the middle managers have the family name Yang, so we refer to the senior person as Lao Yang and to the other as Xiao Yang (or young Yang).

They shoot horses don't they? And eat them out here!

I hope you are all keeping well. Best wishes
Lao Ma Ding (Old Horse Little River)

Alligator for breakfast, lunch and dinner.

WOT'S GOING ON – 11th July 2008

Da jia hao (hello everybody),

The good news is that GKN have finally found a Chinese General Manager who has agreed to take the job and live in Liuzhou. His family (wife and child) live in Canada so he doesn't have the education and cultural issues to resolve, which has stopped many others accepting the job. The start date should be early September, which, allowing for an appropriate overlap, should mean that I will be back by the end of September (just in time for winter!!).

The last few weeks have been very hot and very wet, with several days of flooding, interrupting the factory and making it very difficult to get to and from the hotel. This weather has caused lots of problems with the factory building works and last week we had a major collapse of the newly dug pits (6 metres deep) for our large presses; luckily this happened at night and no one was at the bottom or the situation could have been fatal. We did, however, achieve our half year results, beating budget for sales, profits and cash. The bosses were so happy that they cancelled a visit scheduled for 17th July. I was delighted with that news because it means we can get on and manage the business rather than spend lots of time and effort making the whole site look what it isn't!

Last weekend 3 of us went to visit a minority village 2 hours' drive by taxi and half an hour by boat away from the city. This was a real Chinese tour and we joined up with another group of 10 Chinese people, although we had our own personal tour guide (who spoke no English). We were met at the village by a group of young men and women dressed in traditional costume, playing music and offering us cups of sweet rice wine (very strong). The village was situated at the top of a hill in the mountains, so I was back to climbing up lots of steps again. There then followed the normal dancing and singing (droning more like) that you get with any of these type of tourist visits. They then did some kind of courtship/wedding thing. Apparently you show you like someone by stepping on their foot, if the other person steps on your foot then that affection is reciprocated, the next stage is to hold each other's earlobes and then you are practically married! Anyway it all seems a lot easier and cheaper than what we get up to in the West. We then had lunch of fried maggots, rice, some vegetable thing, pig fat and chicken head soup (luvverly!!).

Then it was off to see some horse fighting!! Best not described but it was an interesting experience, and there didn't appear to be a winner, just 2 totally worn out horses who had managed to cover most of the audience with mud!!! Back to the boat, and back upstream to the taxi. We then split up from the rest of the tourists and went to do some rafting in rubber dinghies: 2 in each boat paddling for 2 hours down a fairly fast flowing river and through several rapids. Obviously we got very wet and had to get in the river a few times to dislodge the boat when it got stuck on rocks. Wet through, we arrived at the finish and got back in the taxi for a very damp 2 hour ride back to the hotel. Not very pleasant! By the time we arrived back my shirt and trouser legs had dried leaving a very obviously damp patch around the middle where the extra layers (pockets and underpants) were still wet. Lots of odd looks from hotel guests and staff as this 'incontinent' big nose waddled through the lobby. No one told us that we would need a towel and a change of clothes, or perhaps we were just useless at the task, and, my excuse, the river was running very fast due to the rains!!!

So yesterday my picture appeared in the city newspaper. The big nose in a boat paddling and seeming to have fun. I'm sure they will use it to show that Liuzhou is a really fun place for foreigners!!! Ha ha, little do they know!

I will be back for a week at the end of July. I hope the summer has kicked in by then!!!

Ma ding

Horse fighting, really quite vicious.

Me and a colleague with some of the minority village people
in traditional dress.

BACK AGAIN FOR THE FINAL STINT!!
(perhaps) – 5th August 2008

After a fairly busy week at home the flights back to China were on time and smooth. Still, leaving home at 5.00pm on Saturday afternoon and getting to the Chinese hotel at 11.00pm on Sunday evening is a pretty tiring journey, OK when I was younger, but much tougher now (like a lot of things!!!!). I now have changed hotel. If you recall from earlier e-mails it took me nearly 4 months to get toast in the mornings and the last week was the final straw!! On the Tuesday evening I had dinner with an engineer over from England and another Danish GKN guy. We ordered our starters, beer and main courses. No problem so far ... The first thing to arrive was the bowl of chips to go with the Danish guy's fish, then the beers came (great!), followed at various intervals by the starters. The main courses for my colleagues arrived before they had finished their starters which is not unusual or a major problem. However my main course failed to appear after ordering it about one hour previously. I was not a happy bunny!! My colleagues finished their meals (no puds for us lean and mean workers!) and I then asked for the bill which was presented with a huge smile by one of the waitresses. I pointed to my main course on the bill enquiring what it was, she explained it was the lamb steak. I then proceeded in my best Chinese to tell her that it might have been a wonderful lamb steak but I didn't have it!! The restaurant manager was called for and did a bit of a Basil Fawlty suggesting it was all my fault and I should have waited a little longer. I said it was all too late now, signed the bill and went off to complain to the hotel manager, who said he was sorry with a non-committal shrug.

The next day I went to look at the rooms in the other (only a 4 star) hotel. Although smaller than my previous room they had been refurbished and looked quite comfortable, and were 20% cheaper. I still was not sure whether to move, but on the Thursday evening, my last meal before flying home I decided to have the beef steak kebab which the Danish chap

62

had enjoyed the night before. Well the meat was truly inedible, I could hardly cut it with a knife and my old gnashers would only move it around a bit. I'm not really the complaining type but I sent it back. It was 15 minutes by the time someone came back to me saying I could order something else, too late again as my colleagues had finished their meals. I decided to walk down town and get an ice cream. So on Friday I booked the other hotel.

So the new hotel. I didn't sleep too well because of the jet lag, had an early bath and then as I was standing in front of the basin shaving, my feet became very wet. The bath water which was supposedly draining away was coming up again through another drain hole in the floor. Great fun as I tried to stop the water flowing out of the bathroom onto the new carpet. It was never going to be easy, this is China!! Reasonable toast for breakfast!! Hurrah! It's the simple things that keep me happy!!

I brought a suitcase full of chocolate back with me to keep the work folks (and me) happy. I only had 3 books, a camera battery charger, toothbrush and toothpaste and chocolate in the suitcase. They do seem to like English chocolate (or is it free chocolate!!).

On Friday, the same day as the official opening of the Beijing Olympics, we will be holding our own silly Olympics at the factory. I have had 350 solid metal medals made for the occasion, one for each contestant. The winners will get prizes of toothpaste, washing up liquid or cooking oil. It's what they value. We've welded and painted some wheels together to copy the Olympic symbol so it should be good fun. I think I've been selected for the ping pong bat and ball race, the equivalent of our egg and spoon. I just hope it doesn't rain.

The current plan is for the new General Manager to start on the 1st September, be with me for a couple of weeks, then he flies to Europe to visit the factories there and meet the key people. He comes back to take charge on the 1st October and I should fly home on the 29th September. I just hope he starts!

It's raining again now and very hot, 33 degrees. I hope summer is with you now.

Best wishes to you all

Ma Ding

My new room for several months, it's narrower than it looks.

OLYMPIC SEASON – 15th August 2008

Several of you have been enquiring about the local company Olympics, so I thought I would send you a quick update.

The morning of the 8th August was very wet so we were all pretty despondent and trying to sort out the contingency plan, which turned out to be using one of the half built structures that at least had a roof. In the event the sun came out in the early afternoon so apart from clearing a few puddles it was hot and dry. Something about sun shining on the righteous I hear you say. I started off the proceedings with a very statesmanlike speech about the eyes of the world being on China today etc. etc. After that we had a quick Olympic quiz. Questions like; who was the Chinese person with the most medals, what is the name of the main stadium, and other stuff. Anyway I handed out a few prizes to the lucky winners. I was under a little bit of pressure to do at least one event. And so to the games proper.

We started off with the 3 person, 2 shoes (planks) relay, a classic event that I'm sure will be included in the 2012 London Olympics. Picture attached. It was organized chaos! We had about 15 teams of 10 or 12 competing so to be fair the organization was excellent. This was followed by that well known race, the 5 legged charge. A lot of cheating in this one so a few teams were disqualified! Then the highlight, the 'blue riband' event, the ping pong bat and ball relay (equivalent to our egg and spoon), balls all over the place, people running across the lanes trying to get their ball back, tripping up others who are not looking where they are going, just looking at their own bat and ball. Great fun!! Unfortunately I then got interrupted by a call from sunny England so I missed the next event which involved 2 people and a long pole, even from all the photographs I still can't understand what they are trying to do! Then to the team skipping time trial; a long skipping rope and teams of 10 who try to do the most skips in 2 minutes. I was sorely tempted to have a go at that but in the end I felt the risk of looking a complete prat was too great. The final event was the tug-o-war. So I had no real choice but to get involved being part of the Admin team against the company champions. Well no ... we lost 2:1, and I think there was a little bit of cheating to help me save face by winning the second pull of three.

The medal ceremony followed. I arranged to have 350 reasonably good quality medals made, one for each contestant, and so the handing out ceremony took quite a long time but was good fun. (Picture attached, now that's why they call us big noses!!) I, of course, refused to give medals to the winning tug-o-war team because I was on the losing side. We then had a little mini tug-o-war with the medals, which again I lost!!! The real prizes for the winners were bags of washing powder, toothpaste and cooking oil. This seems to be the normal valued prizes when they have events like this in China, however I don't think it would work for the real Beijing Olympics ...

The problem with the new hotel is that the only English TV channel is CNN, I really miss BBC World. 95% of CNN is about the presidential election stuff and they haven't even bought any rights to show the Olympics. So my choice to see what is going on is to tune to various Chinese channels, which focus on their own athletes most of the time, or get lucky with CNN announcing another USA medal. In fact the CNN sports headline for most of this week has been 'USA has the most medals'. The fact that China has 16 golds and the USA only 7 is not reported. I noticed this morning that China now has the same total medal tally as the USA, so that CNN headline has disappeared. I have no real idea of how team GB is doing but I can probably guess.

Interestingly, the daughter of my Finance Manager's driver was part of the Chinese gymnastics team that won the gold a couple of days ago. She will get over 1 million yuan (about 80 thousand pounds) for getting the gold medal. This is the incentive that the Chinese team have had in front of them for several years. When you consider that this is equivalent to about 30 years' salary for the girl's father, and it is tax free, and she will still earn more from endorsements etc. you can appreciate why the Chinese team is doing so well. It's also perceived as a way out of poverty for a family, similar to football, boxing and basketball in the West.

Best wishes from your overseas Olympian.
Ma Ding

It's amazing what you can do with wheels!!!

The 5 legged race, one for the strong guys.

Two planks and six feet as fast as you like.

Gold medals for all presented by the big nose boss.

COUNTING DOWN – 4 weeks to go! – 29th August 2008

My replacement should appear in Liuzhou sometime this weekend and start on Monday. Several of the Chinese managers are not convinced they want a Chinese General Manager. They say it's because they like my management style, but I suspect it's really because I don't interfere too much with the detail due to language limitations. Anyway, assuming he turns up it should be better for the company because they need a bit of stability at the top (not that I'm too unstable!!). Karen, my previous assistant who went off to Germany for 3 months and married a 53 year old called Werner, is also due back on Monday. She tells me that she has eaten far too much German stodge and has put on lots of weight. Well she was never a qualifier for the Chinese gymnastics team in the first place so I think she'll have to get back to eating the Chinese fare to lose the excess. My current assistant and Chinese teacher, Matata, has only just begun to understand my strange ways and so it will be difficult to exchange one fairly dainty, softly spoken translator with a loud Germanic one!!! I hope it doesn't Matata too much!!!!

It's all gone very quiet after the buzz of the Olympics. The comments from the Chinese about the closing ceremony are mostly about Boris Johnson being fat and not able to button up his jacket. I was just pleased he didn't speak. There also seemed to be some confusion as to what the British show was supposed to mean, umbrellas and throwing newspapers about!! I suggested that the umbrellas are now used to keep the sun off people's skin in Britain during the summer!! Nothing to do with a wet Olympics.

After a few weeks without any visitors I have now been informed that they will all arrive in a rush the week after next. This includes the new boss of GKN China and another senior China manager, also two big bosses from the UK headquarters. So do I tell them the truth or follow the politics which might enable me to get another assignment sometime? I expect I'll do something in the middle, be a bit outspoken on a few issues but follow the party line on others, it's also not fair on the people I leave behind if I'm too truthful!!! In any case we'll be spending quite a bit of time making the building site look reasonably acceptable. The main problem I have is that if I follow the GKN rules to the letter we would not be able to get any construction work done in China even if the costs were to double, because Chinese contractor companies just don't have the same safety standards as we have imposed on our own workers.

Latest interesting food I've tried included pig's stomach soup, horses' hooves meatballs (like chewing mashed up nail clippings!!!) and frog's bits (but which bits I'm not sure!!). The hotel and food shops are all selling mooncakes at the moment. What are mooncakes, I hear you cry!!! Well in 2 weeks' time we celebrate the Moon Festival. I believe it's a bit like our Harvest Festival in that it's timed to coincide with the end of the growing season and also a bright full moon. These mooncakes are like rice cakes (taste pretty grim) but very nicely shaped and packaged wonderfully; individually wrapped, then put into large silk boxes in sets for the family to enjoy. China, as ever, has a legend that goes with each festival and this one is no exception. This is about the Lady in the Moon, a princess called Chang'e who was banished to the moon for eternity (probably for inventing the recipe for these awful rice cakes!!). There is also a rabbit in the moon as well but that part of the story gets far too complicated. I'm told if you look at the full moon and twist your head so that 4 o'clock is at the top you will see the outline of a rabbit's head. I will not accept any claims for bad necks when I get back!!!

Chinese translation is always a regular source of amusement so to finish I thought I'd tell you of a couple. Having said that I expect our translation of English into Chinese also causes fun for them (or are we always perfect??). Driving out to a restaurant last week I noticed a big Olympic sign outside a shop, but instead of the 'One world, One dream' national Olympic slogan, the printer had got a letter wrong and it became . . . 'One world, One bream', obviously in preparation for the fishing Olympics!!! Also I bought a couple of shirts and only recently noticed the label inside the collar, which reads. . . 'Deducing the classic vogue, creates the unique tasty'. So I guess I can always eat the shirts later!!!

Best wishes

Even if I don't understand the marketing I like the shirt.

RETURNING SOON – 17th September 2008

Well it seems from the news that the world is collapsing around us although the mood in China is still positive. Is it really all gloom and doom back in the UK? No summer, no jobs, no petrol, etc. I have to say; the weather here has been very hot (34 degrees) for the last few days although it cools down a bit in the evening. Anyone want to swap?

Last week I had lots of VIPs visiting from GKN HQ and the new President of GKN China. I gave them all the normal guff and they went away happy, and I even won a couple of issues with my normal tact and diplomacy!!!! The new General Manager started at the beginning of September, spent a couple of weeks with me soaking up lots of information, visiting some important customers and meeting government officials. So with him and the other visitors it's been very busy, not to mention the endless meals of pigs' and chickens' bits washed down with plenty of local beer. Anyway he has now gone off on a tour of the European factories and meeting all the other important GKN people!!! They are really trying to look after him; with good hotels in London, a private limousine to take him from London to Telford, a weekend by Lake Garda in Italy (near our Italian factory) etc. I just hope he stays for a couple of years, he seems a bit like a rabbit in the headlights with everything that is going on. My last couple of weeks in charge should be a bit more relaxing although I will be working 9 days on the trot from next Monday 22nd until I fly out on the evening of the 30th.

Last weekend I took the opportunity to go to Beijing and do the tourist thing, although I had one business lunch on the Sunday. The new Beijing airport (Norman Foster design) was very impressive, a very long walk to the baggage claim area so that by the time I arrived my case was on the carousel. Very clever!!!! My hotel was in the Olympic zone, very smart and only 35 pounds a night. So on the Saturday I did the Forbidden City, Tiananmen Square and the Great Wall. All good fun but too many tourists!!! The security seemed very tight and quite oppressive, this is the first time I have felt the

Party control since I've been in China. I don't really know if this was Beijing normally or just because of the Olympics, but it certainly didn't have the atmosphere of Shanghai or some of the other cities. I even had a real Beijing (Peking) duck on Saturday evening, carved at the table. You may remember from a previous e-mail my utter disappointment when we had Peking Duck in a smart Liuzhou restaurant. It looked wonderful and crispy as it was brought to the table with all the pancakes, sauces etc., but it was only the skin covering some prawn crackers, not one piece of meat! Well the real deal in Beijing had lots of crispy skin and meat. They actually have graded restaurants for Peking Duck, this one was a level 2, they go from 1 (the top) to 4. So organized it's ridiculous.

On Sunday I got a ticket to the Paralympics, general entry to the Bird's Nest stadium. It was only a 10 minute walk from the hotel, lots of security, soldiers everywhere and incredibly busy. The stadium was virtually full and the atmosphere very intense particularly when a Chinese competitor was involved. This was a holiday weekend in China (Mooncake Festival) so lots of people everywhere. I still have no clue as to how the events and competitors are graded, I think you need to study the rule book to fully understand. The women's 1500m was won by a Tunisian who seemed perfectly normal, there were 7 other competitors in the race of which 3 were blind and were guided by male runners. The winner did a 'personal best' time and the second place got a 'world record'. Anyway, all very interesting.

This weekend is Karen's (my assistant) wedding party. It's a bit confusing, she's already legally married to this Werner Hermann character and now it's the big party to celebrate and give them loads of dosh. The tradition is to give a 'hongbao' (red envelope) into which you stuff money. How much? I'm not sure, but as a 'rich' westerner I guess I'll have to find what is normal for a Chinese guest and then use a multiple!!! Many moons ago (last year) I promised Karen that I would give a speech in Chinese at her wedding; well now, to my horror, the time has come and I learned today that there will only be two speeches, Werner's (the groom) and

73

then mine on behalf of the bride. Karen's dad has opted out!!! So I'll do it line by line, first in English, then in my Chinese, then I'll probably have someone else speak in proper Chinese. It should be very interesting. I've also bought a Chinese silk (silkish) burgundy jacket with the toggle buttons etc. so I will look a complete wally. Hopefully it'll take their minds off what I'm saying! After the wedding meal which should finish about 9.00pm, I suspect several of us will go and do the Karaoke thing.

Thirteen days to go. Please can you sort out the weather, the government and the economy by the time I return. Thank you!!

See you soon,
Ma Ding

Karen and Werner in traditional Chinese wedding attire. Very fetching!

Yours truly delivering his Chinese wedding speech to the amusement of all.

ONE LAST TIME – 28th September 2008

Well my bags are packed and I'm ready to go ... etc. etc. Lots of farewell parties have left me feeling a little jaded over the last few days. My final banquet with the senior managers was a very boozy affair but I did manage to make an appropriate speech somewhere towards the end of the meal before my legs gave out. How do I know this? Unfortunately it's all recorded on video. People have been very kind and given me many gifts so that I would remember my time in Liuzhou. So many in fact that I've had to buy another bag to ensure I can get them home.

Talking of banquets, it's interesting that all the food served at Chinese banquets with the exception of fish is cut into mouth sized pieces. The Chinese, along with other Asian countries, see the chopsticks together with the mouth as the main tools for eating. The mouth is used to separate the good bits from the not so good, bones, gristle etc. The mouth dexterity honed over several years can be amazing, a whole prawn going in and after a few seconds the shell, head and legs come out, spat onto the table! We sensitive types in the west have generally lost this ability and use a knife and fork to do this separation duty on the plate, only putting the good bits into the mouth where our teeth will do a quick chew before swallowing. These differences also have an impact on food preparation. For example, the Chinese chef will very quickly chop a whole chicken into the right sized pieces knowing that a combination of meat, bone and gristle matters not since the eater can sort that out. In the west we will carve the chicken, carefully taking the meat off the bone, allowing for larger pieces to be cut up later on the plate by the eater. I'm not sure which is better, it's just different and you get used to it. From my viewpoint I often find myself at banquets ignoring Chinese dishes where I obviously have to do the 'in mouth' thing, since I invariably either spit out too much of the good stuff with the bad, or end up swallowing something I really don't want!

I won't bore you any more with my stories since it'll only be a few days and I will be home to tell you some of this stuff in all its gory detail. I'm really looking forward to getting back.

Best wishes to you all.

A farewell drink with Mr Meng, my Production Manager. The eyes say it all!

The Third Session

Spreading my Wings

Based in the city of Changzhou in Jiangsu Province, a city of about 4 million people just south of the Yangtze River and about a two-hour drive west from Shanghai. As such it is growing very rapidly and more developed than Liuzhou although there are still not too many foreigners around.

E-mails, January 2010 to February 2011

CHINA UPDATE – 27th January 2010

Well I've been back in China now for 2 whole weeks although it seems a lot longer. It is very similar to the early days in Liuzhou (Nov 2006) when there was so much to do to get the business functioning sensibly we were working 7 days a week. I am taking this Sunday off to recover!!

So the business itself is called Shinri David Brown and is a 50/50 joint venture set up to make gearboxes for high speed rail (up to 400kph so not to be used in the UK!!!) and large wind turbines. The investment from the shareholders goes into the bank next week, but so far we have no way of raising purchase orders so I can't spend it. It's a bit like not having your credit cards, cheque book or cash, but you need to buy food. We will find a way round it but I'm having to build up a business from virtually nothing apart from customers wanting product delivered now!

I'm based in a city called Changzhou, about 150 km west of Shanghai and just south of the Yangtze River. Population of 4 million and it seems very spread out and just a big building site. I think most of the pollution is building dust rather than from power stations etc. I have yet to spend time in the city centre and see all the wonderful places (if any) although I've been told there is a Tesco. So weekend shopping at Tesco ... a home from home!!!!

Hopefully I'll get a chance to go into the city centre this Sunday. At the moment there are a couple of engineers here from the UK (Huddersfield) so at least there's someone to have dinner with in the evening.

At the moment I'm staying in a new 5 star Holiday Inn. It is actually very good but it's in the middle of nowhere, or a new suburb of the city which is currently being built. So I'm stuck in the hotel although I'm told the gym and swimming pool will be open soon (maybe!!!). The hotel food is all very samey day after day, but I have an executive room (so there!!!) enabling me to use the small executive lounge which has a happy hour from 6.00pm to 8.00pm every day. This lounge serves some hot and cold nibbles, goodish red wine, beer and some spirits. Some evenings I just sit in there, drink, nibble and read my book. I can't be bothered to go to the restaurant for the same old 'proper' meal.

As ever, travel to work and back is a nightmare with at least one accident to be seen each day. We don't have a regular driver and so last Tuesday we inadvertently got into the wrong car (they are usually black VW Passats, and the drivers all look the same!!!). After a couple of miles the driver had a phone call to ask why he hadn't picked up the clients from the hotel. So we had a strange conversation in my bad Chinese and eventually he agreed to take us to the factory and another driver was sent to the hotel to pick up the others.

I've got to take a quick trip to Hong Kong week after next to get my visa re-stamped. Getting a resident's visa and work permit is tougher now, amongst other documents I even need a criminal record check from the UK, which will take about 40 days and cost the company £300. So I continue to contribute to Prime Minister Brown's coffers!

Hope all is well back in the UK and the snows have all gone. My current plan is to come back for the week 7th March.

Best wishes
Martyn

CHINESE NEW YEAR – 15th February 2010

It's Sunday evening 14th February, New Year's Day, and I'm in a hotel in Shanghai waiting for a very early flight tomorrow morning to Liuzhou. I'm going to see some of my old friends for a couple of days. Actually my old assistant Karen is back from Germany with her husband Werner; you may recall that I gave a speech in Chinese at their wedding in 2008, and they still want to see me! I'm going to visit their new apartment but not sure whether Karen's going to cook Chinese or German food. What a choice; pig's willy or German white sausage, I'm not sure what's wurst!!!

Last Monday I went to Hong Kong for the day to re-stamp my visa. Until I get my resident's visa I must go out of mainland China every 30 days. So unless I'm having a trip home, Hong Kong is the most convenient way of complying with the visa rules. The journey, what a nightmare, probably the worst day of travel that I've ever experienced, 5 hours of flying and 6 hours of delays, and due to bad weather we landed back at a different airport from that planned. Without boring you silly, I'll just say that a Hong Kong Chinese guy named Kelvin, who was also messed around, shared his private taxi with me (we had missed the last trains) back towards my city. I finally got back to the hotel in Changzhou at 2.30am. Happy days!

The English engineers who have been out here helping for a couple of weeks went back home on Wednesday; Bob 'Two Egg' Nabozny and Dave Minor. Bob always has 2 poached eggs every morning and Dave tells me he has an older brother in his early sixties called Maurice!!! I asked if he had an Uncle Colin, but he doesn't!!! (Col Minor).

Last Friday was the final work day for the factory before the holiday period, and just like Christmas Eve in the UK most businesses close at lunchtime, however I had lunch with the big boss of the Chinese JV and someone who had come for an interview. Also every Friday at 4.00pm we have a conference call with the UK, so I had to go back to the office in the afternoon, just me and my Chinese deputy, who has taken the western name Homer!!! However no-one told the building services people that we were going to continue working, so by the time we got back to our office all the power had been turned off for the holiday and everyone else had disappeared. Not only no light, telephone or computer links, but also no heating and the temperature was about minus 6 degrees. It took about 2 hours for someone who had the key to the power room to come back from his house and turn on the power, just in time for our call to the UK.

The gym in the hotel is now open with some wonderful equipment. I bought some cheap trainers and some rather fetching track suit bottoms so I could try to keep fit(ish). Unfortunately the trousers are too short (yes, even for me) so I look a bit of a prat. Having said that, I'm the only one in the gym apart from a clerk who records my room number, time of arrival, etc. Anyway I do a 'cardiac' work out, all electronically controlled; I have to enter my weight, age (old git) and inside leg measurement before the machine gets going. I suppose it's good for me and then I go and have some red wine (which is also good for the heart!!).

Yesterday, New Year's Eve, I went into the city centre to have a wander around. It was very, very cold. I did find a DVD store and bought Avatar to watch in the afternoon, good value for 80p!! The hotel is virtually empty and when I went to the executive lounge on the top floor for my regular wine and nibbles, I was literally on my own apart from the Chinese waitress called Shu Qia, pronounced 'shoe chair'. From about 7.00pm the sky was lit up with fireworks (yen hua in Chinese, meaning smoke flowers); the whole horizon was alight for more than 2 hours. I had the lights turned off and just watched and listened. It was amazing.

The next morning I woke up and the TV wouldn't work, I looked out and there was snow falling and everything was white. Panic, I had to get to the train station and then to Shanghai. I tried to order a taxi but the weather coupled to New Year's Day (equivalent to our Christmas Day in terms of importance) meant that a taxi was unlikely. So guess what . . . one of the bell boys had a friend who was prepared, for a price about 4 times the normal taxi fare, to take me to the station. Well no real choice and I finally got to Shanghai because the trains were running on time in spite of the snow. This is not the UK!!!

I trust you are all keeping well and looking forward to some better weather. I still plan to be back on the 7th March for a week.

Best wishes
Martyn

A firework spectacular by the water.

CHINA LATEST – 19th March 2010

The six days I spent back in the UK went by so quickly and with two days working in Huddersfield I really didn't have enough time to do everything and see everyone I hoped to. Such is life!! My flight back to China was on time and I took the Maglev (magnetic levitated train) from Shanghai airport into the city which this time achieved 432kph (270mph) with only a whooshing sound (the train, not me!!!). It saved me so much time I hoped to catch an earlier train back to Changzhou; however there were no available seats so I ended up waiting for over two hours at Shanghai railway station. Trying to change a train ticket or buy a new one is a real bunfight, thousands of people supposedly queuing but many making excuses that their mother is sick or whatever to get to the front of the queue, sometimes you just go backwards!!

Back into the office after 23 hours of travelling! We are slowly building up the management team and my Production Manager started last Monday and several others will start, including the Finance Director, by early April. Then I will feel that I am running a real business.

As you probably know most of the better educated Chinese have taken an English name, some of the names are pretty ordinary but others are a little odd. So currently in the business we have some normal ones like: Michael, a project manager, Gary, an engineer, and Bruce, a quality supervisor. However my new Production Manager is called Mackson. When I asked why he chose this name he told me it was a shortened form of Michael Jackson! The Deputy General Manager is called Homer (d'oh!) and our HR girl is Daisy (she is nothing like a flower, more of a plum tomato). The new FD is called Jane. So given that China is influencing the world more and more, it might make sense for many westerners to have a Chinese name. As you know my Chinese name is Huo Ma Ding. What would you choose? Hung Lo, Ni Hai, Chu Lip, Zho Li, etc.

A couple of weeks ago my Technical Director, Vincent, who is French, and myself went to look at apartments in the city. Vincent wants to be where the ex-pats are supposed to live, north of the city centre, because his wife will be coming out to join him and she only speaks French. I would prefer something in the city centre where I can use the shops, parks and restaurants. So we were taken to look at 13 apartments in one afternoon, 6 in the city centre and 7 in the north. Well, with all the construction that is going on we hoped we would see something clean and suitable but we were shown tower blocks that were about 10 years old and very poorly maintained. The entrances were pretty grubby, smelling of pee, the lifts were a bit scary and we actually got stuck in one and had to push the emergency button to call the guard to get us out, and the apartments themselves were average. When we went to the northern area we did not see one foreigner. Eventually we lost the will to live and gave up after seeing 11 apartments, telling the agent what we really expected. The only positive thing was that the bathrooms all had 'western' loos and not the normal 'squatty' Chinese hole in the ground that doubles up as a shower!!! However one of the bathrooms we saw was fully tiled with pictures of naked ladies. What is all that about?

In a similar vein; although I have often indicated that the Chinese are good at copying various products and business ideas, they can also be very inventive. As a manager I learned very early on that I would have to be very detailed with instructions because given a little vagueness a Chinese worker would conjure up a quicker, easier and invariably cheaper way of doing the task. This entrepreneurial streak in there somewhere is always waiting for the opportunity to shine. In this respect I was recently in Shenzhen and noticed a new chain of restaurants had sprung up where the owner had clearly seen a gap in the market with a new theme for presenting the food. The name of the restaurant was 'Modern Toilet' where the various dishes are served up in toilet bowls, urinals and potties. Perhaps I am being overly sensitive but I usually don't want to think of where the food will eventually end up whilst I'm enjoying a meal with friends. Why indeed do you need the middleman? It will be very interesting to see whether this theme will take off in other cities or just disappear down the pan!!

The weather is improving and although there is occasionally a cold wind the sun has been shining and the temperature is in the mid teens once the early morning mist clears. I am going to try to get to Nanjing this Sunday, about 1 hour on the train, which was the capital of China before Beijing. For your education; Nan means south, Bei means north and Jing means capital. Nanjing is supposed to be an ancient walled city with museums and lots of parks on the banks of the Yangtze River. It will be good to get away from Changzhou for a day!!!

I hope you are all keeping well, looking forward to Easter and the 'excitement' of the election.

Best wishes
Martyn

A new restaurant established for your convenience.

CHINA LATEST – 6th April 2010

You've had Easter Monday as a holiday and we've had … Tomb Sweeping Day!!! A national holiday when the Chinese pay their respects to their dead relatives, clean the tombs and light fake money etc. to send to their forefathers. I ended up having to make a quick trip to Hong Kong again but this time I couldn't get an easy direct flight to HK so I flew to the southern city of Shenzhen and then made my way by train to the border, crossed on foot and took another train to the centre of Hong Kong. I stayed a night but unfortunately the weather was not too good and then made my way back to mainland China. The current exchange rate makes a huge difference, everything just feels expensive in Hong Kong apart from public transport. I will probably have to go again in a few weeks' time because I am still waiting for the Gloucestershire Constabulary to do a criminal record check on me. One of the many forms I now need to get my Chinese work permit.

Getting back to the hotel last night I was pleasantly surprised to find 2 mid-sized chocolate Easter eggs and 4 Easter rabbits in my room. I am obviously a VIP guest!! The chocolate is white with some strange coloured swirls. You know me, it didn't take me long to take a bite, only to find it's that horrible floury, tasteless stuff you get in cheap sweets in the UK. What a let down, but I really should have known. I will eat it anyway cos choccy is choccy!!

I went to look at a few more apartments a couple of weekends ago. Vincent, my Technical Director has found something in the north of the city and close to all the other ex-pats (not that many) so that his wife can meet foreigners in the same predicament as her (by predicament I mean as a non-working spouse, not just because she is French!!). Anyway the apartments that I preferred, near the centre of Changzhou, although a little better than last time were not really suitable. One was advertised as having both a bath and a shower. The bath was very small and the shower was just a pod that the landlord had installed on the outside balcony without any covering. So the neighbours could look straight in and nearly scrub your back. Needless to say I declined!! I was then taken to the next city, Wuxi, about 45km further East (nearer Shanghai) and it is significantly better in terms of facilities and accommodation than Changzhou. I saw 3 apartments which would have been OK but I now need to find out how long and how much the daily commute would be. I think I will go to Wuxi next weekend and do a bit of exploring.

My new assistant, Cara, started last Thursday. She really does speak 'proper' English and although her work experience is limited I think she is bright enough to cope with most things. The word for translator in Chinese is 'Fanyi'. Cara also speaks some French, so I now share this fanyi with Vincent!!!

I've now set up some Chinese lessons. Once a week as a one-to-one lesson with Dorothy, a big-toothed teacher, and also a Chinese conversation lesson once a week with a German lady who is also trying to learn the language. She looks a lot like Martina Navratilova and is doing some sort of pollution/sewerage consultancy service in the city; well, there's a lot of it about!!! I'm not sure that I would like 'Sewerage Consultant' on my business card, but maybe that works in Germany.

They tell me the weather here will improve during April just as I hope it does for you in the UK.

I hope you are all keeping well and looking forward to the election!

Best wishes
Martyn

WAITING FOR SPRING – 24th April 2010

I expect everyone's got stories of people stranded by the volcanic eruptions, the latest method that Iceland has found to inflict pain on the world. We had a board meeting last week and also several other visitors from the UK, 3 of which are still stranded in Shanghai, one managed to get as far as Dubai and my boss, the CEO, got as far as Helsinki last Thursday and then got stuck. As far as I know he is taking a Norwegian cruise to get to Denmark before driving to France for a ferry back to the UK. He will probably arrive back in Huddersfield by the weekend, maybe 2-3 days after he would have flown back following the restrictions being lifted. What amazes me is that for all the talk of laptop computers and mobile offices so that people can supposedly work anywhere in the world, the moment there is a travel delay they are all desperate to get back to the office!

Last Saturday was a beautiful sunny day and I went for a walk around a large park in the centre of the city. The flowers were out and various musicians were playing Chinese dirges, but it was very relaxing. This had been the first good day in about 4 weeks and wouldn't you know on Sunday it rained all xxxxx day!!! But as I was walking around a lot on Saturday another thing struck me . . . The Chinese pavements usually have two types of paving slabs, one flat and the other with raised parts (ribs or bumps) which are laid down the centre of a pavement so that blind people can walk more easily. A great idea; however, the Chinese have also taken to following the French example with tree lined roads. They put large trees in the middle of the pavements in a raised earth area leaving about 6 inches either side on which to walk. So you find yourself either having to jump into bushes or into the gutter every 20 yards. Not velly clever since there are always many unsavoury items in the gutters!!!

As you know this is a new business that is growing very rapidly and we are constantly trying to recruit people, with new employees joining at about 2 or 3 per week. Anyway a new Production Supervisor, Mr Xu, was due to start on

Monday. He had come from a nearby city, had the right sort of experience and spoke OKish English which, although not necessary in his position, was a bonus. Then early in the afternoon I was told he wanted to leave us. I asked why but no one seemed to have an answer. I talked to him and he said that he couldn't even explain in Chinese what the problem was but he just didn't feel right. I suggested he gave it a week and that we could put him on an extended induction so that he might be able to better make his mind up. He had already paid 3 months' rent on accommodation in Changzhou and we had also paid the necessary insurances etc. However he finally said that although his wife thought he was crazy he just didn't want to continue ... so I said "goodbye" in a not too polite way (using fluent Anglo Saxon)!!! There's nothing worse than a sensitive Chinese production supervisor listening to their inner self (probably just bad food).

Still no luck finding a suitable place to live. You may recall that I'd just about given up on finding something near the centre of Changzhou and had looked at the next city further East called Wuxi. I visited again last week and saw some more apartments, the best one being very near the centre but costing £1,200 per month plus utilities etc. The landlady was not willing to negotiate so I'm going again this Saturday to view a few more. My old IT Manager from Liuzhou (when I worked for GKN in China) Claude Yang is now working in Wuxi so I met up with him for lunch and then he took me to visit a couple of parks. I hope I find somewhere before Julie and Amy get here at the end of May (no, not so I don't have to pay for the hotel; so it will be more relaxing during their visit).

I hope you are all keeping well and not suffering from election fever!!

Best wishes
Ma Ding

Walk on the path and you hit trees, walk in the road and the bikes get you.

MAY TIME – 5th May 2010

I hope you all had a great May Day holiday and are getting ready for the UK election event (ho hum!).

I have now found an apartment in the neighbouring city of Wuxi and if all goes well I should move in during the third week of May. I'm getting fed up now of the hotel and constantly living out of a suitcase, so even though Wuxi is a bit of a commute at least the weekends will be more relaxing. Having said that I will now have to start cooking for myself or going out to eat. Actually I'm quite looking forward to rustling up some sweet and sour piggy ears or crispy goose throat!!! By the time I get back I hope to have mastered a few 'typical' dishes and look forward to inviting you round for a tasting!

I found the local zoo/safari park the weekend before last and so decided to make a visit. As usual I was the only foreigner there and so I was just as big an attraction (no, not attractive!) as some of the wild animals; little Johnny (Zhongy) pointing at me and saying to his Daddy ... "look at that funny man", whilst the giraffe is totally ignored. The zoo had two areas; one was a walkable bit with various cages/enclosures exhibiting the normal flea-bitten animals and reptiles. This included a big, lazy hippo that was close enough for visitors to virtually touch its nose, although the kids and parents bought lots of carrots to throw into its eager mouth. The second part was a safari area where I had to get on a train thing like you get on traditional UK sea fronts. So, with lots of Chinese families eating nuts and stuff we set off for the open areas. We first stopped at an enclosure with several goats, moose, cattle and llamas. There was a man who was selling chopped up carrots for the kids to give to the animals ... not too exciting! Then we moved on and parked next to the lion enclosure, the lions clearly knew that some food was on the way as the train drew up. A man there was selling some chopped up meat which you could buy at 50p a bag. The lions were only separated from us by a narrow stretch of water and close enough for 7 year olds to throw meat to. One child, having bought the bag of meat, was told by his Mum to bring it to her, where she promptly put it in her bag for Sunday lunch; young Zhongy was not happy.

Then on to the next enclosure, the tigers. Again bags of meat were on sale, but as I was standing there admiring these large animals, the guy who was selling the meat got a large white duck from somewhere and threw it at the tigers. This live, flapping duck was quickly caught by one of the tigers and taken away to be devoured, its wings flapping wildly (the duck, not the tiger). The Chinese children loved it. Then on to the wolves' enclosure. Well you've guessed it: the same thing, a live duck hurled at the wolves, who quickly ripped it to pieces. Not the civilised way of the tiger!!! The bear enclosure was next, but no duck this time, they had probably eaten too much already. A very interesting experience not designed for the sensitive children from the west.

As you know we have established this business from scratch and now have about 65 employees, so last Saturday we arranged to have a team-building day for everyone. We set off bright and early in two coaches and 2 hours later arrived at this wooded area next to a lake with a few huts near the lake shore. The event was run by a team who were probably ex-Chinese military since they immediately started shouting and ordering us about. We were split into 4 teams and each team then had to give itself a name, a song/chant and design a flag. I have to say all our employees really got into the swing of it. The highlights of the day were the 'getting a bottle of water' competition and the 'build a bamboo raft to rescue your flag from the other side of the lake' challenge. Needless to say some of the rafts split apart and everyone ended the day very wet. An extremely successful day. This was mainly because the Chinese do know how to balance the serious objective with a sense of fun. Unfortunately the drive back was particularly damp and smelly. I blame it on the lake water!

Wishing you all the best with your election swing-o-meter or whatever the TV techies have come up with this time.

Your man in China.

94

The boss being helped by his team to get a bottle of water without touching the floor.

The rafts not looking too good even before setting off to retrieve the team flags on the far shore.

NO MORE HOTEL – 26th May 2010

I finally moved into my apartment in the city of Wuxi last weekend. The landlady had done all the repairs and sorted out TV, mattress, water machine etc. So the apartment is furnished but doesn't have all the normal items you need to live, e.g. sheets, pillows, towels, plates, glasses, cutlery, cleaning stuff etc. Consequently I spent most of the weekend buying all of the above plus some foodstuffs etc. There is a shopping centre very near with a Carrefour (French supermarket) so I was this strange foreigner going backwards and forwards loaded up with pillows, brushes, buckets, pots and pans etc. Some of the security people had a great laugh at my expense. Anyway I ended up with a bed I could sleep in and a fridge with plenty of ice cream and beer!!! Luxury!

The agent arrived on Sunday with a cleaning lady (known as an Ai Yi in Chinese; sounds painful, doesn't it?) for me to possibly employ. We discussed my requirements (Julie would say how would I know anything about cleaning a house!!!) and agreed 4 hours a week to include washing and ironing as required, all for £25 a month. I then proudly showed the cleaning materials I'd bought only to be greeted by lots of tut-tutting. It was decided that the best thing to do was to let the cleaner go and buy the correct stuff there and then. 30 minutes and £18 later and I'm sorted!! I only hope she turns up on Thursday and does a good job.

I am sharing the lift to work with a young Swedish engineer called Hannes who works for one of the sister companies on the same site. However he normally finishes work by 4.30pm or 5.00pm whereas I don't get away until after 6.00pm. We are using his taxi service in the mornings which takes about 45 minutes with a very careful driver using the normal national roads. In the evening I'm using a driver and car that we will probably employ long term and it takes 35 minutes using the motorway including a £1.50 toll. So not too bad considering that if I were to have found a flat in the north of Changzhou (where a lot of the ex-pats live) then it would take about 40 minutes to our factory in the south of the city. One highlight, on the way in to work today we passed an old open-back truck with some guys in dark uniforms, huddled together but each holding instruments, a Chinese brass band on tour!! I gave them a good stare as we drove past. Anyway at the next traffic lights they came up alongside us and started playing some Glen Miller tune (Pennsylvania 6-5000 I think). Maybe they were after money from the rich Swede!!

The latest trend in China seems to be for young women to wear glasses without lenses, large dark frames but no glass. What is that all about? Have you seen the same thing in Europe? Or am I missing something fundamental here or just getting old?

I did manage to get to the World Expo in Shanghai as a guest of one of our suppliers. The queues were incredible, any pavilion worth visiting required a wait of at least 30 minutes. I did get to see the UK, Spanish, Luxembourg, Swedish, Croatian and Turkish pavilions of which the Spanish was by far the best. I also went into the big African pavilion where all the small African countries like Mali, Botswana etc. had smallish individual exhibitions. You know how it is when you are on some faraway beach relaxing and an African always comes up with a tray of beads, carvings, or other useless stuff to sell. Well they never miss the sales opportunity because all areas of this pavilion had small stands selling this xxxp. We were also lucky enough to get a group ticket to see the Chinese pavilion which is about 10 times the size of all the others and incredible. I don't know how much coverage you are getting on this Expo thing but it is the big news in China.

Julie and Amy come out for a visit next week so I hope the weather holds and all the arrangements work out OK. We are relying on public transport and my limited Chinese to get around and eat so it could be interesting.

I understand summer has started in the UK with plenty of BBQ opportunities. I will definitely miss the outside cooking, although I might rig something up here on the balcony. It'll give the natives some additional amusement!!

Ma Ding (now in his own home)

My 24th floor apartment in Wuxi, clean and modern!!

SIX MONTHS IN – 17th June 2010

We've just returned to work after celebrating Dragon Boat Festival. As ever in China the story that underlies the reason for the holiday has made sure that there is opportunity for some form of display and something different to eat. The story goes that about 300BC a guy named Qu Yuan drowned himself in protest against a cruel tyrant. His supporters raced their boats to the place where he drowned and threw rice dumplings into the river so that the fish would not eat his body. This has now developed into boat races in most cities and the gift of these sticky rice things wrapped in vine leaves. Just like the Spring festival, the Company handed out presents to all employees; so I got a washing up cloth, some shower gel, a box of semi-cooked duck eggs and a box with 10 of these sticky rice in leaves things. I will try to cook one in the next few days but my memory of eating one of these a couple of years ago is not good, aching jaw and dodgy taste!!!

Julie and Amy visited earlier this month and as luck would have it the weather could not have been better. I had put together a pretty tight schedule so that they could visit the famous places in Shanghai and Beijing. It all seemed to go reasonably well with only one delayed flight and the Shanghai Expo just being far too hot and packed with people. The queues for most of the popular pavilions were over 2 hours long, so we gave them a miss. The best was the Malta pavilion because it had a small bar where we sat and drank some cold beer for a while.

Julie and Amy managed to buy a few things to brighten up my apartment, however I had a real problem with 3 small pictures to hang on the wall. No nails or hooks supplied. I went to the apartments' maintenance dept. and explained what I wanted but the best they could do was 3 smallish screws. Well I tried the Chinese method and hammered one of the screws into the wall but it just made a big hole and wouldn't stay in well enough to support the picture. Next I went to some shops selling pictures and explained the situation, but it seems they don't sell picture hanging hooks either. I eventually got some large nails from work, cut them in half and bashed them in. It worked ... bodger Ma Ding strikes again!!!

World cup fever has hit China and one of the TV channels seems to be showing most matches even though the timing is not great. I suspect China will make a bid to host this event in the not too distant future. It's not just the TV, there are posters and displays in most shopping areas and I walked into a hotel lobby the other day to be confronted by a 10 foot tall cardboard cut-out of Wayne Rooney, not a pretty sight!!! Luckily I was able to dribble round him and a Ronaldo cut-out without losing the ball!! We'll wait to see if England produce a reasonable display, but I'm not getting my hopes up and neither is my French Technical Director about his team.

I had to travel to Qingdao last Friday to attend a quality meeting with our customer and the end user (Beijing Metro), we have a few niggling issues to sort out. I also needed to be back in Changzhou for a meeting on Saturday morning so we had arranged a late flight back (11.40pm) to Shanghai, a hotel in Shanghai and a driver to pick me up at 7.30 am. Qingdao is supposed to be a beautiful city on the coast between Shanghai and Beijing. It was where the Olympic sailing events were held. Anyway we drove for 7 hours to get there (no available flights), had the meeting and then the customer had organised a big banquet at a famous seafood restaurant. No way to refuse and as I was the foreigner I was asked to go to the fish tanks to make the selection. Not a big problem, however there were some really horrible looking things which I declined but were served up anyway. The chap next to me at the table bit into something that looked like a big fat oyster with a double trumpet coming out of one end. As he bit in a whole load of muck jetted out of the trumpets all over the table. Nice!! I was also expected, as ever, to do the main drinking on behalf of the Company. Although I did have the excuse of flying later I managed to survive but I am now apparently the 'brother' of some big fat smelly Chinese guy from Beijing. The flight was nearly 2 hours late so I didn't get to the Shanghai hotel until 3.00am, didn't sleep and so was not in the best of moods on Saturday. Never a dull moment!!! I really need a relaxing weekend.

I hope everything is tickety boo in the UK and the new government is fixing all the problems so that by the time I return there are jobs and milk and honey for us all.

Best wishes
Ma Ding

A VERY WET SUNDAY – 11th July 2010

Well the big news at the moment is the weather. I hear you've had a great couple of weeks in the UK with plenty of beer and barbeques. It's been well into the 30s here and very sticky with it, however this weekend has been very wet. Wuxi is one of the cities in the Yangtze flood plain and if you've had the news coverage you will know that there has been horrendous flooding all along the Yangtze, particularly the provinces just west of me. In fact over 400 people have been killed so far in floods and landslides and still the rains continue.

I was on the train back from Shanghai the other day and the man next to me was trying to read his newspaper but obviously some of the print was too difficult for him to focus on because he kept moving the paper backwards and forwards. Then as one of the attendants came up the aisle he asked if she had any reading glasses. I thought, this isn't a normal request for a train attendant and I could imagine the response from a UK train ticket inspector. Anyway she politely responded that they didn't have any. So being the friendly foreigner and since I often carry a pair of reading glasses with me, I offered mine to this chap who was incredibly grateful. He started talking very loudly, thanking me profusely. Unfortunately I didn't understand everything he was saying, so a woman across the aisle started acting as a translator and soon several people were listening to our 3 way conversation. In truth all I wanted him to do was use the xxxx glasses and read his paper. Eventually it all calmed down, he read the paper and when I got off the train about 40 minutes later lots of people were saying goodbye to me, hopefully thinking the Brits are not too stuck up.

We take safety at work very seriously and I have introduced a process for reporting accidents and near misses, which I thought was very clear. However after several months without any incidents I finally had notification of a near miss. When asked what had happened I was told that one of the workers had cut his finger. We then had a debate, with me saying that it was a real accident because the guy was injured and the production manager convinced that it could have been much worse, so it was a 'near miss'. I remember when I started running the previous Chinese company they designated a broken leg as a minor accident!! We just have a different perspective on these things.

I bumped into a westerner in the lifts of my apartment block a few days ago. It turns out he is from West London out in China on a 4 year contract working for Lloyd's Register of Shipping, based at the port on the Yangtze about 20 miles north of the city. He is in his mid thirties and his English girlfriend works in Shanghai so he goes there every weekend. However when he is not at sea he is around during the week so we've arranged to go out and have a beer or two. I've learnt that he pays 50% more than I do for the same size apartment. Maybe he has other benefits that I don't, I'll have to ask!!!

Yesterday I had to go to the Post Office to send some documents to the people who are sorting out my work permit. Saturday morning and most of the counters were open and no queues. I used my best Chinese and the girl seemed to understand, saying it would cost about 9p and then if I wanted secure delivery (the guy next to her helped with some English on this one) it would cost 35p. I chose the latter, she put the stamp on for me and put it in the appropriate pile behind her (I hope). I was only in there for less than 5 minutes with great service. It can't all be about low labour cost, it's also about attitude and people grateful to have a job. I only hope the letter will arrive safely.

Only one more week and I'll be home for a few days. I'm really looking forward to it and breathing some fresh Cotswold air; however I expect the time will go quickly and I'll be back in the land of the Zhong guo ren (Chinese people) before I know it.

Best wishes to you all.
Ma Ding

BACK IN CHINA AGAIN – 5th August 2010

As most of you probably know I had a quick trip back to the UK last month, firstly to attend Amy's graduation and secondly to get a 'Z' visa which enables me to get my Chinese work permit and resident's visa. It was great getting back to Painswick and seeing (or not seeing) the clear air.

However as many of you know, the Post Office used their very expensive and efficient (sarcasm with a big ladle) 'Special' Delivery system to lose my passport and visa documents for 3 days. Without going into all the gory details, by using favours at the Chinese embassy and express courier riders, I received my passport back in my hand at Heathrow airport about 10 minutes before I checked in for my return flight to China. Not good for the blood pressure!!!

Back to work and it's incredibly hot, about 35-40 degrees most days. Julie has come back with me, no, not to cook and clean as I thought, but to relax for a couple of weeks before her holiday to Bali and her return to teaching sometime later this year!!!! The pace of business here does not let up and we have now produced our first high speed gearbox and large wind turbine gearbox. These are now being tested before going into full production in the next few weeks. Some of the test instrumentation shipped out from the UK couldn't stand the heat and kept blowing fuses, so we've had to buy a special cooler and several large fans to simulate UK temperatures in our workshop. The roof of the workshop leaks badly so when it rains I now have a little area of China with English weather (cold, wet and windy)!!

I was due to take the train back to Wuxi the other day and sat across from a middle aged businessman in the waiting room. He was wearing a dark suit and tie, black shoes and socks and holding a smart briefcase, but because it was so hot he had rolled up his suit trousers to expose most of his lower legs to keep him cool. He started to engage me in conversation in Chinese and of course I told him what I was doing etc. However the legs were not good and I had to concentrate hard to stop myself looking and laughing. It is a regular thing to see Chinese men with trousers rolled up or shirts rolled up to expose their stomachs in order to get the air flowing on hot days. Not very pretty!!!

You may recall from my last letter that I met an English guy living in the same apartment block. His name is Keith and he has been good enough to take me to 3 different bars in the city over the last couple of weeks. The nearest to the apartment is called Havana and is run by a Spanish couple, it's more of a wine bar, quiet with a very limited menu. The other 2 are run by Australians. One is called the Blue Bar run by a very large Ozzy with a 'crush your hand' g'day hand shake, the other is called Ronnie's run by a toothless drunk who props the bar up whilst his Chinese wife runs around looking after him! Both of these Australian bars have reasonable bar food and are quite lively with several ex-pats hanging around. However these are the type of ex-pats that I really don't want to meet since they are usually loud, fat and continuously moaning about what's wrong with China and going on about what's wonderful with Germany (the ones I met were all Germans). This wasn't helped by the World Cup football result against England. Anyway it gives me some other places to visit when I'm bored.

The team standing in front of our first wind turbine gearbox built in China.

A couple of observations from Julie regarding the changes in China.

1. Julie feels that eating with a "couple of twigs" (chopsticks) will be a distant memory in a few years' time. With more and more restaurants offering American fast food or Western style menus with knives and forks, the Chinese are moving to metal eating irons rapidly. I have to say that at work many of the younger employees take their own spoon to the staff canteen to eat their daily gruel rather than use the well-worn wooden 'twigs'!!!

2. You can regularly see older people squatting by the side of the road smoking a ciggy or watching the world go by. For us they look very uncomfortable, but they have had many years sitting on very low stools, using squatting loos etc. so their muscles are used to this position. Julie's second observation is because the current generation use normal height chairs and there are many more western style loos, the Chinese will soon lose their ability to squat!!! A great loss to world culture!! I suggest you try squatting for a few minutes to feel some new muscles.

These may be small changes but hundreds of small changes add up to a big cultural shift, not always for the better.

I hope you are all having a great summer wherever you are.

Best wishes
Ma Ding

A kerb-side squatter.

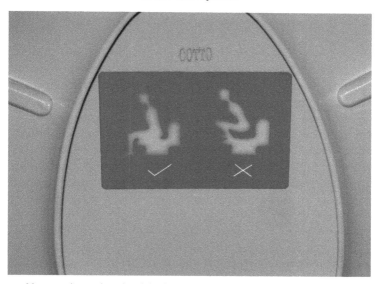

Note on the underside of the loo seat showing how these new-fangled western-type toilets should be used.

NOT IN BALI – 28th August 2010

As I write Julie and Amy are enjoying the delights of Bali and some of the nearby tropical islands. Am I jealous?? Yep. However when they were talking about improving their tans it occurred to me that there's got to be a central global marketing consortium persuading different races to continue to purchase skin products. Turn on the TV in Europe during the run up to summer and it's all about getting bronzed and protecting your skin from the sun's harmful rays, in winter it's keeping your tan using spray-on products. Turn on the TV in Asia and there's loads of adverts for skin whitening products and once you get to the appropriate shade of white there's products to sustain it. I've always been a bit cynical about marketing but I'm now convinced this skincare stuff is organised on a global basis.

The latest news from Changzhou is that we're running out of power. It is possible that the city is developing faster than the utility supply. So from today industrial sites will have 5 days of reduced power. In fact it's going to be 5 days' reduction in every 14, and it looks to continue for at least 2 months. We have written to the government to say that we are a priority business, but I suspect most companies are doing the same. (It might eventually come down to banquets and drinking to establish priority companies.) We will just have to alter our shift patterns to match the power availability, another little local difficulty. Having said that, all the city buildings will continue to be lit up like Christmas trees.

I thought I was going to be clever introducing a continuous improvement programme at work. Simply put, different members of the management team would do a patrol of another area and note down things that could be improved, the point being that fresh eyes see new opportunities. This would include all parts of the business. Anyway one of the improvements that arose was filling some cracks in the office walls and painting them. So we got a typical family team (Tang, Bong and Sun) in to do the work. Well, they filled the cracks and did the painting. Unfortunately they also splattered paint on the floor carpet tiles. So we had to call them back in to clean the carpet; this they managed to do but not without damaging the skirting boards. So, you've guessed it, they had to come back and paint the skirting boards. No, they didn't get too much paint on the carpets this time!!! However what was supposed to be a continuous improvement activity turned out to be continuous work. It was all a bit like a Charlie Chaplin film!

No doubt you've all heard about the terrible mudslides we've had here in China. We did a company collection for the victims. The Sunday of last week was an official national day of mourning. What was amazing was that all 68 TV channels, including CNN, HBO, were all showing the same programme about the mudslides, the victims, the rescue work etc. This one-hour programme cycled continuously all day on every channel except the one Chinese News, English language channel, which basically showed similar things with an English commentary. This is the first time that I've seen the state control the media in this way. It did focus our thoughts on the tragedy.

I've become a common sight in Wuxi now so I don't get all the stares and only the occasional 'harro'!! Well it's either they've got used to seeing me around or my eyes have gone a little darker and my skin changed to the local hue. I'm still undecided about buying a bicycle. It sounds a good thing (keeping fit and getting around easily) and the bikes are not expensive, but the traffic and driving are really bad. There is a completely different attitude to road use here in Wuxi, i.e. anyone can use any part of the road (or pavement), pedestrians or any type of vehicle; traffic lights and lanes are for guidance only (red for go but look around a bit, amber for go and sound your horn and green for go go go!!!). Nobody has right-of-way so everyone can do basically what seems right for them, no need to look behind, the following vehicle will probably take evasive action, hoot a lot for no particular reason, and if it does end in a jam or a crash just abandon the car before the police arrive to make matters worse. Anyway it's been far too hot for cycling, I'll wait for the weather to cool a little before deciding on the bike.

The Chinese partner, who is also the Chairman of our company, has decided to buy a local competitor and will expect the English partner (David Brown Ltd.) to stump up their share of the purchase price so that our joint venture shareholding remains at 50/50. This acquisition has about 480 employees (we have 70) and so the plan is to move our business onto the larger site, integrate the 2 businesses and thereby very quickly create a stronger capability and larger market share. I will be the General Manager of the new entity which is located a little further west of the current factory. I now have 2 weeks to put the integration plan together.

I hope all is well in the UK and the economy is thriving!!! I have really missed the summer barbeques.

Best wishes

Power cuts in the factories but still the neons shine.

WINTER IS COMING – 18th October 2010

I'm now firmly ensconced in the new factory. It's a huge place with big offices, marble floored corridors and enormous factory workshops. Unfortunately it is further away from my apartment in Wuxi, but as yet I'm not sure how far. So my driver, Wally Wang (he drives a bit like a wally!!), and I are trying lots of different routes to and from the office. It's no good using maps because the city is developing so rapidly that there are no up-to-date maps. The best we've managed so far is 50 minutes (I know that if I was driving it would be less!!) and we are still trying to get approval for the automatic toll collection which would save another 5 minutes. The bright spot is that as we arrive at the factory gate the security guards, recognising the car, stand to attention and salute me. I have to bite my lip so as not to laugh. I'm obviously expecting the same respect from my family when I get home next time (some chance!!!!).

The problem with the long marble floored corridors in the office building is that you can hear the echoes from a long way away and this being China various people choose to clear their facial passageways regularly and loudly. It always stops me in mid-sentence when the noise starts, but my Chinese colleagues just accept it as normal practice. My temporary office has what can only be described as a Louis XVI three piece suite in dirty mustard yellow and various other assorted furniture which is probably from the early MFI period and very wobbly. It is also opposite and above the canteen so from mid-morning there is a bit of a whiff … ahh the canteen!!!! I thought the previous factory canteen was bad enough with metal slotted trays and dollops of unidentifiable stuff, however even my workers are complaining about the small quantities and quality of this new canteen. I have eaten there once and have decided to stick to cup-a-soups and fruit from now on. When we fully take control we can sort it out so that at least half the food is recognisable as coming from the ground, sea or animal.

The local supermarkets seem to have themed sales events, a bit like Tesco or Waitrose having a wine festival a couple of times a year. So a few weeks ago just prior to the national holiday there was a major push on suitcases, back packs etc. This week seems to be national foot bath and massage equipment week!! Throughout the local stores there's lots of promotional shouting and music extolling the virtues of a good foot massage with live shows, prospective customers putting their smelly feet into the modern (plastic) appliance for a good bashing, locals pointing at the lucky victims and eventually some walk out with a big box under their arms and a bigger smile on their faces. Just wait till they get it home and plug it in!!! I wonder what the next event will be . . . a home chicken feet extractor and stewer!!!

I was in a local hot-pot restaurant the other evening and it was quite full of people. Suddenly there was a big commotion coming from behind a pillar in the middle of the restaurant. A couple that were hidden from my view were obviously having a big disagreement (she probably wanted fried rice and he wanted boiled!!). Then the people at the nearby tables quickly got up and moved away as plates, dishes, cups and chopsticks started flying around and breaking on the floor. The waiters and waitresses rushed across, some felt it was too dangerous and quickly ran away again whilst some braver ones tried to catch some of the flying crockery, I saw one clever waiter nearly catch a cup, juggle a bit with it, then unfortunately drop it!!! At least he tried. Luckily I don't think the main food had been served so the couple quickly ran out of things to throw and so fled the scene shouting at each other, then the clear up began. Well that was more exciting than the food I ordered which was pretty bland even though it was cooked in some table top barbeque thing.

Although we've recently had a few sunny days it's certainly getting colder in the mornings and the evenings, winter is definitely on the way. In fact it feels a bit like good late autumn UK weather. I'm looking forward to coming home for a week at the end of the month and hopefully catching up with some of you then. Best wishes to all.

The main office building that also housed the apartments for visitors.

General Manager's furniture for greeting visitors and the occasional lunch-time snooze!

ODDS & SODS – 12th November 2010

I've just returned from a quick, but enjoyable week at home. Julie had worked hard to arrange things for my time at home, including booking the people to fit a new gas boiler and the builders to do some repairs to the roof. So British workers at their best ... the plumbers turned up with the wrong boiler and had to go away and order the right one; the builders eventually turned up, erected their scaffolding and went away again. Then it rained so they couldn't work for the rest of the week!!! This would be totally unacceptable in China, most things get done when you want it done, the only danger being they sometimes do it too quickly and the quality is not necessarily the best. The UK will never be able to compete. Maybe I should bring a gang of Chinese workers back and set up in competition!!

Jessie, one of the girls in the office got married last week. Prior to that she brought in, as tradition demands, a small red carrier bag for everyone with choccies, various bits of chewy stuff and a couple of boiled eggs. I obviously swapped my eggs for chocolate. She then had her wedding and I was told it was a very grand affair with over 500 guests. So I assumed that she came from a wealthy family to be able to pay for both the Chinese style wedding (Civil ceremony, red costumes and parties etc.) and the western-ised version with white wedding dress, top hat and tails. Lots of photos and a big banquet. Not so, in China it's the groom's family who pay for all of this!! So being a father of two girls my feeling is that I should adopt some of the Chinese culture for any future family weddings!!! I know that several of you are in the same boat with girls who will be getting married in the next few years. Shall we gang up and change the rules???

We've had a few bright, clear autumn days recently but today driving to the factory from my apartment was really odd. There seemed to be some form of inversion which formed a layer of pollution just above chimney height. Instead of smoke going up and dispersing, it was going up about 20 feet and then moving horizontally where it would meet up with other pollution and form a thick dark layer of crud. Not nice and I could taste it at the back of my throat!! Hopefully it'll burn off when the sun comes out.

As I've mentioned before the two sounds that will always remind me of China are the traffic horns and hawking/spitting. The daily commute of nearly 2 hours a day has allowed my mind to wander. So I've been doing some analysis of the way drivers use their horns. It's not straightforward and I've noticed a regular pattern (how sad, I hear you say). The double quickie (beep-beep) is reserved for pedestrians and means 'beware, I'm coming through'. Then there is either the short-long or the single long (beep-beeep or beeep). This is reserved for other car or truck drivers and means 'beware, I'm behind or beside you so stay in lane' (many drivers have a tendency to wander across lanes for no reason). The third is the continuous beep and is used in a particular case. Let me explain ... There are lots of traffic lights with left and right filters. If there is a normal red traffic light and you are going straight on then normally (unless you are a big truck, taxi or motorbike) you should stop. However if you are going to turn right and there is a red light then there seem to be two schools of thought. One is to stop and wait for the light to turn green, the other is to just turn right and force your way into the traffic that is coming at right angles. So the continuous beep is used when someone has stopped at the red light but the other drivers behind want to turn right; in this case they all gang up and use this continuous noise to force the driver at the front to pull out into crossing traffic and cause all sorts of other problems. It's bad on the ears but oh it's fun to watch!!!

There is one other use of the continuous beep which is reserved for mourning. As you know in the west we have 2 minutes' silence at times of national mourning. Well in China a time of national mourning is marked by as much noise as you can make, which includes car horns. This was particularly in evidence during the Sichuan earthquake 2 years ago and the landslide disaster earlier this year.

Unless any of you are particularly interested I don't think I will do the same analysis on the different hawking/spitting sounds!!!

With this acquisition the rules have changed to force us to work at least *every* other Saturday. This is because the new company we are acquiring normally works 6 days a week and we work 5, so the Chairman has decided for harmony we will all work (550 people) *every* other Saturday. This is obviously causing a problem for the original team who joined a company working 5 days a week and have other commitments at the weekend. I'm also not best pleased!!!! Anyway only a few weeks before I'm back for Christmas.

I hope you are all keeping well, best wishes
Ma Ding

SEASONAL THINGS – 28th November 2010

About 2 months ago I was invited to a banquet with about 15 other people, hosted by our JV partner company in a really good restaurant in Changzhou. I was one of 5 foreigners in the party. We had a fish/seafood meal cooked with individual hotpots, like having your own personal fondue pot. Anyway towards the end of the meal, when we had consumed quite a few drinks, a camera crew turned up and started filming us. They asked if one of the foreigners could say a few words in Chinese. Unfortunately my colleagues started pointing at me and I couldn't easily back out. So I recited a few phrases as requested and then returned to eating, drinking and normal conversation. I forgot all about the incident, but last Monday when I arrived at work several folks told me that I'd been on TV several times that weekend advertising a restaurant. I'd been conned!! So I offered a percentage for anyone who can get me some advertising fees or a few free meals at the restaurant. Highly unlikely I think!!!

Still on the subject of advertising, Christmas is now being advertised widely in a lot of shops in the typically Chinese tacky way, lots of big plastic Father Christmases, reindeer and snowmen. Even though the Christian religion is followed by a very small minority, when it comes to a commercial opportunity the Chinese never miss a trick. We had lots of visitors this week and therefore a couple of large banquets. At one of these I was sitting next to one of my managers who had somehow found out it was my birthday the day before. Again, the Chinese never miss an opportunity and here was the chance to sell some of the 'traditional' Chinese 'birthday noodles' known as Chang Shou Mian (literally long life noodle). So everyone was served up a small bowl of spaghetti swimming in a horrible brown sauce, most had one mouthful and forgot it, but they did all get up and sing happy birthday in a mixture of English and Chinese. Same tune, different words.

You will probably recall that over here there seem to be fixed times to force sell various items, some linked to partic-

117

ular festivals, like the dreaded moon cakes for the mid-autumn festival and others like suitcases or footbaths because it is that time of year again. Well it's now winter thermals time!! Everywhere shops, department stores, market stalls and folks on bicycles by the side of the road are selling one-piece or two-piece thermals. It has to be said that they do seem to come in a wide range of colours and patterns, so if you are interested (extra large in lime green with pink polka dots for the boys??) get your order in now before they all disappear and we move on to the next big thing. My guess, it'll probably be a new cooking device for crispy pig's face!!!

The so-called under-floor heating in my apartment has been playing up. The local plumber arrived last Sunday with one big spanner and a hammer, he then borrowed a bucket and after about an hour of banging around and with various Chinese curses he pronounced that it should now be OK but would take a few hours to heat up the floor. He charged me £8 for the work and the heating seems to be OK but I think it is probably a better ceiling heating system for the apartment below me than it is an under-floor heating system for me. There is only one control; on or off, so today I bought a small oil-filled radiator and a separate timing clock to make sure the apartment is warmish when I get up in the mornings and when I get home from work in the evenings. At weekends I'll turn the under-floor system on because it takes about 10 hours for the heat to come through. We take all our modern heating controls for granted in the west. Also I'm sure I am one of the lucky ones who has a heating system installed and can afford to have the heating on a lot of the time. Which brings us neatly back again to why now is the season of thermal underwear!!!

Apart from a small plague of cockroaches in my office at work there is not a lot else to report. The TV has been full of China winning thousands of gold medals at the Asian Games held over the last 2 weeks and a new apartment block has opened about two hundred yards from me. In the normal way when a family move in they let off lots of fireworks to scare away the bad spirits. So just about every evening for the last week I've had a great view of wonderful firework displays.

Only four weeks to go and I'll be back for Christmas. I hope to see some of you then.

Best wishes
Ma Ding

Spicy Prawn Heads ... no tail flesh anywhere to be seen. Not as crispy as it looks and the brains just squidgy.

HOME FOR CHRISTMAS … MAYBE???? –
22nd December 2010

As I sit here today I'm not sure whether I will be able to get back home for Christmas, it seems that the weather is so bad that only some long haul flights are working but even if I get back to Heathrow will I be able to get to Painswick? Oh yet another adventure!!!!

My apartment block has been 'tastefully' decorated with big Father Christmas faces on the doors, cardboard cut-out Christmas trees and various fairy lights dangled over several bushes in the garden area. At least an effort has been made even if in daylight it looks pretty naff. Most of the staff in the shops and restaurants are wearing red hats with white bobbles on them and big cone shaped constructions are popping up all over the place with lights on them. I think they are supposed to look like trees, but actually look a complete mess and because they are just plonked down randomly they are causing a combination of pedestrian and vehicle congestion, not helped by the fact that most people ride their motorbikes on the pavements. Bah humbug!!!

We've had a couple of days with really bad pollution which you can feel at the back of the throat. The only benefit is that the sunsets are incredibly colourful with a huge red sun as it goes down and because it's been the time of a full moon, it too looks huge and is a bright orange/yellow colour. However I would happily exchange the colours for some good, clean Cotswold air, even if it is extremely cold at the moment. The new factory is about a mile from the lake so we generally get better air quality than the other industrial areas although we often get misty conditions giving a damp feel to the air.

My driver, Wally Wang was not a happy Chinaman the other day, he'd closed the car door on his thumb and the nail had turned a bright blue colour. Now, when I've done this (very rarely, I might add!) my nail has turned a purple colour. So I'm thinking what's the difference in the blood, or is my driver somehow connected to the British Royal Family (Wally Wang

Windsor? Did Charles ever visit China in his younger days??)? It was his gear changing hand, so for a couple of days the drive to work has been even more interesting as he is using his other hand to change gear and not able to grip the steering wheel whilst doing so. Consequently for each gear change we do a little swerve across the road. This has largely gone un-noticed by the other road users because it is so normal for vehicles to wander across the lanes all the time. I hope it gets better soon and we can revert to the normal level of danger!!!! We did have the power shut down in our district all of last Friday and were only told about it the day before. So, most of the factory workers had the day off in exchange for working the following Sunday. I was in wearing as many layers as possible but my hands were so cold I had trouble writing. Driving back in the evening, it was interesting that although none of the traffic lights were working, it was not necessary to have a policeman to direct traffic as we would have in the UK; everyone just carried on as normal weaving their way across the junctions with the occasional small prang!!

Every month the UK business has a senior management meeting based in Huddersfield and all the overseas bosses are expected to call in for the duration of the meeting. It starts at 10.00am UK time and usually lasts for between 4 and 5 hours, so 6.00pm to 11.00pm China time. The whole thing is a real pain, particularly arranging to get back to my apartment late at night. However this month I decided to try our own local facilities. The office block in the new factory is basically a U shape with 4 floors. One leg of the U is normal offices on all floors. The other leg has the canteen on the ground floor, nothing much on the second and accommodation for visitors on the 3rd and 4th floors. Probably about 20 rooms in total with an executive suite into the bargain. So you've guessed it, I decided to try the executive suite, finish the conference call at about 11.00pm and walk the 30-40 yards to the room. I had a look at the room, which really comprised a single bedroom, shower room and a double bedroom/sitting room. It had various large damp patches on the wall where the paint had peeled off and was a bit grubby but I was assured it would be cleaned up. Well I duly finished the meeting which included eating some pot noodles for my evening meal, then went to my room. No hot water, the bed was solid and the room heater (an air-conditioning unit) was noisy and incapable of heating the room. I had a very uncomfortable night, cold shower in the morning and no breakfast. The benefit of waking up an hour later than normal was completely wasted, and I was in a grotty mood for the rest of the day. I now have to think of a better plan for next month's meeting.

Latest news from the odd food front: last week I was out for a meal and the menu had a list of dishes including some pictures of the favourites. Asked if I wanted fish, I said 'yes fine'. Well they ordered something called 'fish bubbles'; it looked like white flaky fish in the picture. However when it arrived it did look a bit like curly white bubbles. I tasted it, pretty chewy and tasteless. It turned out to be fish gills. It's not likely to go on my list of the 'must have' Chinese dishes!!!

Wishing you all a very Happy Christmas and fingers crossed I'll be home to have a small dram with some of you.

A top notch individual hot pot meal with prawns and various sliced meat (seen at the back). My favourite type of Chinese meal.

PARTY TIME – 19th January 2011

Xin nian kuai le! (Happy New Year)

Well, I obviously managed to get home for Christmas, the only problem was the total incompetence at Heathrow Airport in finding somewhere for the plane to park and getting our bags. It took two and a half hours from landing to getting out of the airport!! The time it took coming back into China, from landing and queuing up to go through immigration to getting my suitcase and getting out, was only 40 minutes. However it was great to be back home, even for such a short time, and Julie had spent a lot of time preparing some wonderful food (enough for several weeks as usual) and making the house look very Christmassy, so after eating the good stuff and all the choccy I have come back to China a little bit heavier.

Now it's the run up to Chinese New Year and everyone has gone mad. The shops are selling all the red posters and hanging stuff, red lanterns are popping up everywhere and all the shop assistants have swapped their Santa Claus hats for red and gold uniforms. I guess it's just like the run up to Christmas with people buying all sorts of food, drink and other stuff that they wouldn't normally touch at any other time of the year, and they buy enough for three weeks even though the shops are only closed for one day!!! Madness. The prices of most things have gone up a bit (particularly for delicacies such as goose throat and duck tongue!!!) and the queues at checkouts are really long; it seems that the only time I can go to my local supermarket and not queue for too long is first thing on a Sunday morning, all other times it's a heaving mass with lots of arguments, shouting and shoving. I might be several thousand miles away but some things just feel the same.

The boss man of our Chinese shareholder held a big meeting/party on Saturday to celebrate the results of last year and tell everybody they've got to do even better this year!! This session was held in one of his new factories that hasn't got any machines in yet, a huge empty shed. About 3000 employees were invited with lots of tables, plastic stools to sit on and some sunflower seeds to nibble (parrot food?). I turned up and was invited onto the podium with nine other bosses to hand out various prizes to worthy employees. It was soooo cold, about minus 4 degrees; when people came up to the podium and collected their prize I would say congratulations (in Chinese) and there would be a big ball of hot misty breath coming out of my mouth which was accentuated by the floodlights, all very odd in the photographs. This section of the meeting went on for about an hour interspersed by several boring speeches. Then we all went to our seats in the audience to watch some shows and sketches performed by the employees … and this went on for three hours!! Some of it was quite good with big indoor fireworks, but it was so cold my extremities (and I'm sure everybody else's) were frozen. The torture finally concluded and then a group of about 200 of us went to a hotel for the evening meal, which as ever ended up being a drinking session. I chose to stick to the red wine, a classic Blue Nun cabernet sauvignon which is all the rage in China now! And yes I ended up with a bad head-ache, I think the last glass must have been off!

There are three of us foreigners (an Englishman, a Swede and a Japanese) in my apartment block who all have drivers and leave at about the same time every morning. Our three drivers now seem to be good mates, sharing ciggies and if it's raining they all sit in the Japanese guy's people carrier and I'm sure have a good laugh at us stupid foreigners. Luckily Wally Wang (my driver) has been told not to smoke in our car, but I don't think the Japanese guy minds if his car is full of smoke from time to time. The cold and wet weather has made driving even more hazardous with cars skidding all over the roads. We pass at least one accident every day. The cyclists and those on the electric bikes are wearing so many clothes to keep warm, including scarves and hoods to keep their faces free from the icy wind, they really cannot move their heads to see the traffic around them. Unfortunately I've seen a few very serious accidents involving these electric bikes since they disregard most of the traffic lights but cannot see or avoid some of the heavy traffic. Even when it's dark most of them don't turn their lights on so they can save electricity and drive a few extra miles.

At the moment I'm sitting in a cold office as again today we have a power cut. It has been snowing overnight so it took me just under 2 hours to get to work this morning and because snow is rare in this region they have no idea how to drive in these conditions. It would be funny if it wasn't so dangerous and I'm sitting in the passenger seat with Wally getting us into some potentially sticky situations so the whole thing is pretty stressful. We passed 4 bad accidents this morning with cars and trucks overturned.

Back to the power ... the whole area is out for at least today but we do have a company generator which should keep some lighting and computers working although no heating at all (yes, more misty breath). The only good news is that I can cancel some of the long, boring conference calls with the bosses in the UK.

The wife of Vincent, my French Technical Director, gave birth to a little boy on Christmas Eve in a hospital in Shanghai. He said that they experienced hospital care superior to anything they would have expected in France, so obviously much better than the UK. They have called their little boy Noah. I think they are hedging their bets seeing all the flooding problems around the world at the moment and hoping that as parents they will be first on the ark!!!!

I trust all of you have recovered from the excesses of Christmas and are still keeping to your New Year resolutions!

Best wishes
The cold man of Changzhou
Ma Ding

Can't criticise the sentiment but the spelling could be better!!

VELLY INTERESTING!!!! – 27th January 2011

Just a quick note to let you all know that I've been caught in the middle of a company reorganisation. Good news and bad news . . .

David Brown Ltd now have two businesses in China, one based in Shanghai and my business based a couple of hours to the west in Changzhou. As I've mentioned before we have recently acquired a bigger business and are just starting to make it work in an integrated way. Because this new business is fully capable it has been decided to close the Shanghai business and transfer some of the employees to Changzhou. Yes, you've guessed it . . . there are now two General Managers in China, one who has worked for David Brown for over 20 years and myself, so I'm the one who will be 'redeployed'!!!! I've been on the other end of this a few times so I know the routine but I've never had it happen to me, so it's another new experience!!!

The good news is that by the end of February I will be back home, the bad news is that I probably won't have a job (or is that good news as well???).

At the moment I'm fairly relaxed about it and we will see what the reaction is when we make the announcement in the next couple of days. So I'm trying to ensure a smooth transfer to the new GM, something I've always done during my interim assignments, and organise the move out of my apartment and shipment of my personal belongings to the UK.

Time to de-rust my golf clubs and think about buying a car.

Best wishes
Martyn (formerly known as Ma Ding)

FINAL MISSIVE – Until next time!! – 10th February 2011

The news of my departure met with mixed responses; the people who I had recruited in the original business were shocked and disappointed, whereas the people who we've recently acquired just think it's another management change and are still really waiting for the disruption they've had over the last few months to settle down. Anyway they didn't have to ponder the implications for too long since the Chinese New Year holiday arrived. However two days before the break we had a major problem in the business caused by the big Chinese boss and his New Year gifts to employees. This year we had a box of dirty apples (quite tasty when cleaned), a vacuum packed goose with all the bits and a box of milk. The day after these were all given out I was sitting in my office when there was a commotion out in the corridor, sounding as though loads of women were shouting and arguing. I went to have a look, and sure enough there were about 30 of our female workers clearly very unhappy about something. This something, I found out, was that the Chinese boss man, in his largess, had also given out vacuum cleaners to all the staff and some, but not all of the other workers. There seemed to be no explanation why some people had got these and others hadn't. (I didn't get one, just content with my goose bits!!!) To cut a long story short, the following day several of the workforce went on strike, we called in the local employment bureau chief and the police to help. The biggest problem was that there is no real union or party representation in the company, so there's no one to negotiate with, just a rabble. As usual with these situations, ring leaders became obvious and more vocal, so we eventually were able to find a solution by giving a financial equivalent to the vacuum cleaner, however the 'unfair' and unthinking management style of the Chinese partner has left an unpleasant feeling across the business.

The Saturday before Chinese New Year my Chinese teacher invited me to a friend's house for a dumpling dinner

128

and to play Majiang (mah jong). I eventually found the apartment in a pretty run down part of old Wuxi, lots of bars on all the windows. I was warmly welcomed by my teacher's friend (Mrs Wei) and her 7 year old daughter. Hubby was at work as usual. Another teacher also turned up with her young Korean male student. The apartment was very small with a small kitchen and dining area, a bathroom off the dining room and 2 small bedrooms. I was then told I had to help make the dumplings before we could eat. There is a real art to making these things so they hold the mixture in and look appetizing as well. I'm not sure what the inside consisted of, it was greenish brown with some white bits. I was told there was pork and vegetables and some other things. Best not to think about it too much!!! So at first I did make some strange looking dumplings but then settled down to produce the proper size and shape. Maybe next time we'll have a DIY dumpling party in Painswick!!! Following dumplings and dumpling water to drink (Julie has experienced this before, not her favourite) we played ma jiang. This event took place using a mixture of Chinese, Korean and very little English. I hadn't played for a couple of years but eventually surprised them by winning although I left the event 3 Rmb down (about 30p)!

Last weekend I travelled down south to Guilin to meet up with some of my friends from the GKN business. The weather was much better, 22 degrees and sunny. We watched the big firework event on the Saturday night, unfortunately we couldn't get very close because of the mass of people but it was incredibly impressive lasting continuously for about 35 minutes. I was told that the city had spent £300,000 on the fireworks; considering they are about one quarter of the price we would pay in the UK, it would be more than a million pounds going up in smoke!!! The next day we visited a park with lots of monkeys and went to a hot spring in a town about 20 miles north of Guilin. We decided to have an early evening meal and had a selection of about 6 roadside restaurants with all of their wares out on the street, fish, various live animals, snakes and vegetables, even a small dog already gutted. The safest bet seemed fish and so we chose a couple of catfish-looking things which were promptly pulled out of the tank and killed. To be fair everything was piping hot and very edible, washed down with a few beers. With all the food quality scares that we regularly hear about in China it's sometimes comforting seeing and eating totally unadulterated fare.

Andy, one of the GKN engineers who was with us (his surname is actually Beer!!!) told me that the GKN business is now on its 5th different General Manager since I left in 2008. Clearly not only David Brown has trouble with senior management stability in its Chinese businesses.

Now back in Wuxi/Changzhou I've been woken up for the last couple of days by fireworks, even earlier than I would normally wake up (6.15 am) to go to work. This is the Chinese tradition of chasing away the evil spirits from their homes and businesses, or is it using up all the left-over fireworks that are being sold off cheap after New Year celebrations? The first few days back in the office I've been sorting out my files etc. for a smooth transition to the new General Manager, having my photo taken with several of my staff who want a picture with an old foreigner and having some farewell lunches and dinners. Over the next few days I will be packing up my stuff and sorting out all the utility bills and banks etc. I really hope the bureaucracy of getting out of contracts is easier than signing up for them in the first place or I will never get out of China.

Anyway, all being well I should be back home for week beginning 20th February, just in time for Julie's half term holiday. She tells me that the list of jobs is now on the second page . . . and there was me thinking I would be having a rest . . . Help!!

Best wishes to you all, see you soon.
Ma Ding (soon to be known as 'Martyn the unemployed')

Me and my monkey.

A typical road-side restaurant. Choose what you want from live fish, small mammals and birds (in the cages) with various odd veg. Find a seat and eat.

Farewell banquet with my management team.

The Fourth Session

Almost my Second Home

Hangzhou is situated about one hour south-west of Shanghai and is a well-developed location with many western businesses, including well known hotels, supermarkets and restaurants.

E-mails, August 2011 to June 2012

HERE WE GO AGAIN! – 6th August 2011

Yes I'm back in the land of the dog stew and goose throat delight!! After a fairly uneventful journey I arrived in my new home city of Hangzhou where the temperature was (and still is) in the mid 30s (90ish F) and with very high humidity. Hangzhou is situated about an hour by fast train (if it doesn't crash) south-west of Shanghai, about the same distance away as my last assignment, just further south. However Hangzhou is supposed to be reasonably civilised and is famous as a holiday destination for the Chinese due to its historic West Lake and famous green tea. At the moment however it looks to me like many other big Chinese cities with lots of high rise buildings, lots of construction and jammed with cars, bikes and people. Maybe when I've had time to explore I'll find the differences.

My role this time is to train the new General Manager who is a Brit, having worked for the Group for about 20 years and the Chinese business for the last 2 years. He has been promoted to the role of General Manager, doesn't speak much Chinese and has very little experience of finance, purchasing, sales etc. but does know how to make wire rope. That is what this company produces: wire rope for suspension bridges, cranes and mining equipment. In fact the big arch on the new Wembley stadium is held up by this company's wire rope. Steve (for that is his name), the General Manager, seems to be a good guy, very enthusiastic and quite imposing (6 foot 3 inches and over 20 stone). We are both living in this up-market apartment complex about 20 minutes' drive (in the morning, 40mins in the evening) from the factory and about 25 minutes' walk to the lake. My apartment is the same size as my previous apartment in Wuxi but costs three times as much. I guess that's the price of a civilisation!

There are power restrictions in various Chinese cities at the moment which means that many businesses have to stagger their working week. We are not allowed to work on a Monday so currently we work Tuesday to Saturday with Sunday and

Monday as the weekend. I'm writing this on Friday evening, work tomorrow and then I'm really looking forward to Sunday when I can sleep and catch up with the jet lag etc.

Because I haven't been able to go shopping yet for food and provisions for the apartment, Steve and I have been out to eat every evening this week. His name is Steve Weston and in line with his name he only likes 'western' food, so we have been to some of his favourite restaurants, mainly American and Italian so far. Now I understand why he is so big; if I carry on like this I'll come back 4 stone heavier. Soon to be known as 'lardy Marty'!!!

Other characters in the business include Casey who is the General Manager's assistant. She speaks pretty good English, is 7 months pregnant so waddles around the place. She expects to leave about one week before she gives birth and return almost immediately since her mother-in-law will look after the baby. Thank heaven for mothers in law!!!! If you've got a good job in China you will always try to keep it.

Albert is the Sales Director. He is a Hong Kong Chinese who is probably about 60 with jet black hair and a chain smoker. He has been with the business a long time so although the rules are no smoking in the office no one has had the courage to stop him filling his office with fug. He seems a bit of a law unto himself and he has an arrogance which is typical of the Hong Kong Chinese. Sales levels are a problem at the moment so I will have to put him under a bit of pressure in the next few weeks. It'll be interesting.

Anyway, my first week is nearly over and I'm quickly beginning to understand the size of the challenge. It was never going to be easy and the key at the moment is to conserve as much cash in the business as possible until we can increase the customer orders. Oh happy days!!!

I trust you are all enjoying the wonderful British summer.

Your man in the East
Ma Ding

My apartment at £2,300 a month. That's typical for Hangzhou,
similar prices to London.

NEARLY ONE MONTH GONE!! –
25th August 2011

Doesn't time fly when you're busy? I've been back in China now 4 weeks and so I've just about settled down into a bit of a routine: Up at 6.00am, in the factory by 7.20am, then have a cup-a-soup or sandwich (made by myself!!!) around midday, then leave at about 5.30pm to get back about 6.15pm. The Saturday working should finish this weekend and so from next week I hope to have the normal Saturday and Sunday off ... whoopee!! Since I've been here the weather has been incredibly hot and humid (about 38°C), however in the last couple of days it's turned into a British summer; overcast, rain at times and about 24 degrees, quite a relief from the heat. At least I don't have to shower and change every time after I pop out to the shops.

Last week I was doing a quick search of my new (if a little scruffy) office and I discovered a 3 quarters finished bottle of Chivas Regal 18 Year Old whisky. About £50 a bottle. Obviously the company rules don't allow alcohol in the factory so I have offered to take it back to my apartment and dispose of it. This I have done quite happily for the last few evenings! The apartment complex has got quite a good gym, with most machines having a dedicated TV or music player, and also an indoor swimming pool, so in order to offset the whisky I have tried to get to the gym two or three time a week. That's OK although I have noticed that some Chinese come in, sit down on a machine and just watch the TV; even the gym attendants can't get them to do any exercise. But I guess they can tell their parents, wife or doctor that they did go to the gym for an hour! By the way, although the swimming pool looks OK it is often very busy with locals swimming incredibly slowly round in circles or sitting on the edge smoking and frequently spitting into the pool, so I've given it a miss so far.

Hangzhou is a bicycle friendly city. Every 400 yards or so there is a communal bicycle station where about 20 bright red bikes are lined up, with the front wheels locked in a pod thing. People seem to come along, take them, cycle off and others arrive and put bikes back continuously. I now understand; you pay about £15 for a card, which also acts as a deposit, you swipe the card next to the bike which releases it, then you can use the bike for up to one hour without charge, or about 10p for a full day, then take it back to any other bicycle station in the city. A good system used by many. Now the weather has cooled down I will either buy a card and use the communal bikes (but you don't know who has last sat on it, do you!!!) or maybe buy my own bike; the shop up the road is selling what looks to be reasonable bikes for £17 and the apartment complex has an underground lock-up.

Banking ... what a farce!! HSBC (Hong Kong & Shanghai Banking Company), my bank in the UK and in Shanghai. Now I'm in Hangzhou and there is an HSBC branch about 5 minutes' walk from the apartment. I am thinking ... very easy for all my banking needs, transfer some GB pounds to my Chinese branch then get it changed into local currency. With a local HSBC branch ... no problem? So last weekend I went to the bank with Steve (who also banks with HSBC). I wanted to transfer £2000 from my foreign currency account to my Rmb account. I even rang my personal banking manager (Ken Long) in Shanghai to ensure there would be no problems. Trying to keep the story short ... no, they couldn't transfer this money for me, I would have to go to Shanghai. Or ... and this is what we had to do in this modern age of electronic banking: the cashier very carefully counted out and gave me £2000, I then handed it to Steve (we are both leaning on the counter in front of the HSBC cashier), he then gave it to her to pay in to his account, she carefully counted the notes again, Steve then requested a cash withdrawal of Rmb20.000 (£2000) and she carefully counted this out and gave it to him, he handed the wad of notes to me and I gave it to the cashier to pay into my account. She carefully checked the amount again (as if we were magicians who had managed to make some notes disappear in front of her eyes). Finally she confirmed that I had the Chinese currency in my account. We had no money in our hands when we walked in and no money when we walked out, so, tired and bemused, we went for a beer. At least I now had some money in my account to pay for it!!!

I have to go to Hong Kong this weekend to get my visa stamped since I am only allowed to stay in the country for 30 days at a time. I am in the process of getting a new work permit and resident's visa. So last week I went for the medical and this week I had to get some more passport size photos for all the documents that are needed for this process. I was taken to this little shop thing and I went into the back room for the photograph. The young photographer only took one photo. We then went to the front room where he sat in front of a computer, pulled up the photo on the screen and proceeded to modify it. Firstly I had my head slightly tilted to one side, so he disconnected my head from my neck, straightened my head, reconnected it to my neck and smoothed the edges of the neck. He then got rid of a few loose eyebrow hairs, lightened my cheeks a little, softened the bags under my eyes and smoothed out some wrinkles on my chin. All in about 3 minutes. I paid him the £2.50 and went away with 8 photos of someone who looks a lot better than I do!!!! One day they'll be able to do all the work on the real person in 3 minutes and then take a photo!!!

I hear the British summer is living up to its normal high standard. Well at least we won the cricket.

Best wishes
Ma Ding

Bicycles and electric bikes everywhere in the city. Petrol motorbikes are banned in the city centre.

AND SO IT CONTINUES ...
– 15th September 2011

I have now moved to another apartment in a different building, but in the same complex. This apartment is a bit bigger but much lighter with the living room having one long wall of glass and another large window on the side. The sun comes in during the morning and heats the place up so the air conditioning is vital. This place has a separate kitchen area and I've even started using the oven to slow cook the meat so it can be cut with a knife. Most of the pork and beef is fairly tough to eat if it's just stir fried, which is my normal cooking method ... just get loads of ingredients including garlic and ginger, chop them up, put them in the wok thing, cook on a high heat which splatters everywhere, then eat. Only one pot and a plate to wash up ... easy!! One of the other good things about this city is that I can get some foreign TV channels, including ESPN and Star Sports which is actually showing all the Rugby World Cup games live. Being only 3 hours behind New Zealand means that I can watch them live. The other 'bonus' is that there is no commentary available, only the referee's mike and the stadium tannoy. So I can have the choice of sitting in my room with a drink watching on my own, stretched out on the sofa, or I can go to the bar for 'happy hour' and see who's around, although there is always the risk of some local wanting to watch Kung Fu or Ping Pong!!

We are trying to recruit a new Finance Manager and the Regional Human Resources Director has got us working with a recruitment firm in Shanghai. The two managers we deal with are Lilly Wong and Molly Gong (the truth) and their English accents are so bad that on the phone you never know if you're talking to a Wong or a Gong. (I often get it Wong!!!) In fact with some of the people they've sent us to interview I often wish I had a gong to hit to finish the interview quickly when it's obvious the candidate is a waste of space. We also need a Sales Manager and a Quality Manager so we're running a bit thin at the moment.

Hangzhou, although mostly famous for the 'beautiful' West Lake, has a large river running to the east of the city. This river is called the Qiantang (qian means thousand and tang means soup???) and has the largest tidal bore in the world apart from the Amazon. Apparently it makes the River Severn bore look like a mere ripple, ninety people got washed away last week (none drowned) because they got too close. So I thought that since the best time to see it is between 5th and 15th September, last weekend (10th–11th) would be great timing. Steve (the General Manager) who currently has his wife and mother-in-law staying with him (as if he doesn't have enough strife at work!!) also thought this would be a good idea. So off we set on Sunday morning allowing plenty of time to get stuck in traffic and arrive before the expected tidal bore time of 1.30pm. Well we parked and walked up to the side of the river which must be more than a kilometre wide and looked down from the concrete river bank onto the muddy, swirling water. There were a few other locals standing around and our driver then started having a conversation about when the bore would actually pass by this point. It was felt that 3.00pm was a more accurate time. Steve got our translator from work on the phone and after a while it was all agreed that 2.30pm was the right time. Now there is a big, new, modern shopping mall within about 5 minutes' drive of where we were so it was decided (Steve's wife decided!!) that we could spend an hour there, have a sandwich for lunch and get back by 2.15pm. This we did only to clamber up the river bank and be told by some smiling natives that we had missed this world renowned spectacle by 5 minutes. I was not a happy chappy!!

Talking of drivers, we have two; Mr Shen, also known as Munki, and Mr Yang who is always referred to as Mr Lost. Steve and I usually use Mr Shen, who drives the 6 seater Buick people carrier. His driving style can only be described as aggressive. It is not unusual if some other driver cuts in front of him for the retaliation to start. Steve and I are wanting to get back to our apartments after a hard day at work and Munki wants to play chicken with other drivers, pulling in front of someone who's upset him and stopping at a green light so the guy behind can't go, then at the last minute just as the light turns red we pull away and the guy behind doesn't. Frightening!!! Our other driver just lives up to his name and seems to have no sense of direction, can't read a map and is always late. We will have to sort this out.

And another thing (moan, moan, moan), two weekends ago I had to fly to Hong Kong to renew my visa. As usual I had a window seat where I can keep myself out of the way during this two hour flight. Sitting next to me, in the middle seat was an old lady with a major tooth (or lack of) problem and sitting in the aisle seat was her daughter who was also carrying her baby, probably less than six months old. Then in the seats in front of me were two young lads about seven or eight years old who seemed to be travelling on their own since the man who was sitting in the third seat next to them very quickly asked to be moved. Well it was obviously the first flight for these two lads because they were exploring all the buttons, window blinds up and down and being very boisterous, looking over the back of the seat to see this odd looking foreign man. Granny next to me was on her mobile phone as we were taking off, shouting to be heard above the roar of the engines, in spite of being told to turn off mobile phones, the baby was screaming and the boys in front were up out of their seats. You get the picture; the crew were nowhere to be seen as they were buckled up safely at the front. Once we'd leveled off granny proceeded to persistently slap/massage her right shoulder, regularly looking at me with a toothless grin. The lads in front had found the air hostess call button above their heads and were delighted to regularly push it, listen to the 'ping' and wait for one of the crew to come and ask what was wanted. Sense of humour failure was becoming evident. Without giving chapter and verse of the complete journey, the final straw was that the mother then proceeded to change the baby's nappy using the back of seat table normally used for eating the in-flight meal. Needless to say when the chicken bits with rice were served I was not very hungry!!!

After a relatively cool week of 30 degrees the temperature has climbed up to the mid/high 30s, so it's a lazy weekend for me watching the rugby. I hope you are continuing to enjoy the great British summer!!!

Best wishes
Your man on the lake.

A view of Hangzhou City from across the West Lake. The lotus flowers and famous Broken Bridge.

MA DING ON WHEELS – 2nd October 2011

Yes, I've finally done it and bought a bicycle to get around the city. After visiting a few shops and supermarkets I finally bought it at the local equivalent of Tesco, a chain called Century Mart (sounds like my age!!). Plenty to choose from including fold-ups, rounded handle bar with basket types, road racing bikes and mountain bikes. I went for a bit of a mixture, a mountain bike thing with shopping rack on the back, comfy seat but big tyres and a few gears, all for the sum of £50. You can imagine the looks, this old foreign chap riding around inside the shop to test the bikes. The shop assistants seemed to enjoy the event. As ever in China nothing is simple and as I've probably told you before, once you've agreed to buy the thing, the assistant writes out a multi-part form which then needs to be taken to another separate cashier (not the normal check-out tills), you queue up to pay and then get back 2 of the forms with some glue and stamps on, return to the place where the bike is, hand over the forms, more stamps and you get one form back and the item you have bought, in this case a bike. Now at this point I thought I would be able to exit and ride back to my apartment. But no, I then had to walk with my bike (I decided not to ride it) from the far corner of the supermarket up and down the aisles to the check-out tills and then queue up with people buying their normal rations of rice and chicken feet etc., finally present my receipt to the check-out girl (and it's not easy manoeuvring a bicycle through the check-out) to finally exit the shop.

After all this excitement I decide to take a gentle ride back to the apartment (about 10 minutes). But yet more fun and games; after cycling for about 5 minutes there was a click, click, click from the front wheel. I stopped and looked only to find a short, fat screw protruding from the front tyre. I pulled it out and the air started hissing so I quickly screwed it back in again. Now in China there are lots of little road-side repair places and I knew of one about 200 yards from my apartment, so I decide to ride there as quickly as possible before the tyre went down. I got near to this place just as the tyre was getting flat and actually walked the last few yards puffing and sweating. I showed the old guy squatting on a little wooden stool outside the shop my problem (the puncture that is!!!) he said OK and proceeded to throw my brand new bike flat on the pavement and got a couple of old screwdrivers to take the tyre off without removing the wheel. He was very efficient as he brought across a bowl of dirty water (maybe his lunch-time gruel) and dunked the inner tube in to find the leak. Rather than watch my brand new purchase get abused I decided to go into the shop across the road and buy a loaf of bread. When I got back the job was done and so I asked him "how much?" After paying him the equivalent of 40 pence for his endeavours I rode off only to find, as I nearly ran into the cyclists in front of me, that he hadn't reconnected the front brake. You just can't get the service nowadays, or I guess you get what you pay for!!!

You may recall from my previous e-mail that I was not best pleased to miss the world famous Hangzhou tidal bore. This message seemed to get back to the person who manages the drivers so it was decided that the following Saturday we would try again, recognising that the bore would be somewhat smaller. Steve had gone off to Shanghai for the weekend so it was just 'me and my Munki' (as in the song title!!) the driver who went to see the spectacle. The estimated time for the bore to pass was 3.30pm so we left my apartment in plenty of time at 2.00pm. The driver decided to go a little bit further away than last time for a better view. We arrived at 3.00pm, clambered up the bank only to find that it was actually happening there and then. I quickly got out my camera to do the tourist bit. The bore didn't stretch across the whole 2km width of the river but was very impressive all the same and must have been about 3 metres high as it passed, with lots of follow up waves making some large barges swing around violently. Less than five minutes later we were on the way back.

To all readers from Windlesham (where we used to live before going to France and then back to Gloucestershire), I am living in an apartment complex called the Oakwood Residence. To get there in a taxi it needs to be pronounced Ow cur woo duh. I'll try to bring back a Chinese sign for all of you living in Ow Cur Woo Duh Road, Windlesham.

The weather has turned decidedly autumnal, colder and drizzly (although still above 20 degrees). So the umbrellas are out all over the place and I have my own weapon!! I'm convinced that pavements need to be made one way for pedestrians because it is just downright dangerous walking against the stream of people all carrying umbrellas. Because (believe it or not!!) I am taller than the average Chinese, my head and eyes are at umbrella spine height for others carrying, so I must also carry one to protect myself. And then you have the umbrella dance ... as you approach a line of people walking four abreast with umbrellas at the ready, your eyes meet and then at a distance of about 3 yards, the brain cells start to consider the options; umbrellas up, down, left or right, then everyone makes their move ... Only to find you've both done the same so can't pass, you both quickly react to take the opposite position so still can't pass and eventually just barge through to lots of expletives or step into the road where the electric bikes blare their horns at you. So I'm voting for one way streets for pedestrians or a mandatory umbrella users' licence!!!

This weekend (1st and 2nd October) is the National Holiday in China, second only to the Chinese New Year in importance. A lot of people have gone to their family homes for a few days and have tacked on a couple of their 5 personal holidays (not the 25 we get in the UK) to make a decent break. However, working for a British company that doesn't care for what is culturally important to Johnny Foreigner, we are having to work during parts of this holiday to ensure the September results are provided to HQ on time. So I will be working this weekend and hope to have a day or two off sometime next week.

I hear you have a mini heat wave at the moment. Enjoy it since it probably won't last. I look forward to seeing some of you when I get back in three weeks' time.

Ma Ding (the bike-man of Hangzhou, now repaired)

My trusty steed with fully sprung frame and telescopic forks, all for £50.

ALL CHANGE AND FIRST CRASH –
14th November 2011

Another week begins and for my sins I have been made Managing Director with a 2 month extension to my contract, so now I should get back home end of March. Not bad really since it gets me home in time for spring. The previous MD, Albert of the jet black hair, has gone back to doing what he does best; wheeling and dealing in Hong Kong. So I now have to pick up the reins and try to sort out the sales force, the grimmest and most demoralised bunch I've seen for a long time . . . a real challenge!!!!

Amy was with me all last week and we went to see the Panda Research Centre in Chengdu, Sichuan province. Lots of pandas of various sizes living in near perfect conditions. We were really lucky with the weather and went very early in the morning to beat the crowds and hopefully catch the animals being fed. I think Amy took about 500 pictures which will be on her Facebook site (whatever that means!!). Although I have been before in 2007 this was a much better visit since it was far less crowded and the sun was out. The previous evening we met up with my Chinese teacher from Stroud who with her husband Mark (she is Chinese and he is a Stroudy!!) has now moved to Chengdu. 5,000 miles away and we meet up with someone from down the road, what a small world we live in!!! We all went out for a spicy mushroom hotpot in a mist filled restaurant with condensation dripping from the windows.

Earlier in the month I had my first bike crash. Now let me get my excuses in first. As you know most of the inner city roads in China have about 8 lanes, 3 going in each direction mainly for cars and motorbikes, and a bike lane each side supposedly for electric bikes and bicycles, then obviously a pavement each side. Apart from the pavements most drivers/riders go in the right direction, but there will be a small proportion of bikes in the car lanes and cars in the bike lanes, as well as cars, electric bikes and bicycles on the pavement. In fact if you are riding a bike (motor, electric or pedal) and want to go in the opposite direction to the proper flow, and you can't be arsed to cross to the other carriageway, it is easier to drive on the pavement and force pedestrians to get out of the way!!! You get the picture. So I'm riding along in the middle of the bike lane (yes, in the right direction), there's a line of slower bicycles on my inside and electric bikes and motorbikes on my outside, it is very busy and you just go with the flow. Well one female pedestrian several yards ahead decided to step into the bike lane, the elderly lady cycling on the inside ahead of me swerved to avoid her and I had no real choice; either swerve into the motorbikes outside me or crash into the old lady cyclist, which I then did with aplomb. We both ended up on the ground in a tangle of bikes and limbs. I got up quickly, pulled my bike up out of the way and tried to help the old (about 60ish???) lady to her feet. She was screaming and shouting and wouldn't get up, the lady who stepped out into the bike lane and caused the problem turned to stare not really knowing that it was her fault. I picked up the other bike then used my best Chinese to explain that it wasn't my fault. The police looked on, as did several other people. I finally got the lady to her feet and she quietened down and seemed OK. Then a sudden realisation came over her as she obviously thought that she could get some money from a rich foreigner. She started to complain about her thumb at which point I decided to say it was all her fault, got on my bike and rode off. The police didn't want to get involved, no money in it for them!!!

I have a Chinese lesson one evening every week which usually includes about 20 minutes of general chat in Chinese, then some reading from text books and some other varied learning. Like a lot of languages there are many idioms or phrases in common usage in China which express particular meanings and there are surprising similarities between English and Chinese idioms. For example we say 'it's no use closing the stable door after the horse has bolted'. The Chinese equivalent is 'don't close the sheep pen after the sheep have wandered away'. Another one which amused me because it reflected some Chinese personal behaviour is their equivalent of 'to be green with envy'. The Chinese translates as 'to have a three-foot length of spittle' (i.e. drooling); sums it all up really!!!! There are many others of a similar nature which I can bore you with some time.

Another bit of culture for you to practise at home is the Chinese method of hailing a taxi. In London the style is to hold out your arm and shout "taxi" as loud as you can. In China we start by holding the arm straight out as in a Nazi salute (are you trying this?) and then begin rapidly flapping the hand from the wrist as quickly as possible keeping the fingers locked. This only works if a taxi is in the vicinity otherwise you just look stupid!!!!

It seems we are in for a period of bright but colder weather in Hangzhou and it's certainly getting chilly in the evenings; as long as it doesn't drizzle I'm OK. I trust you are still all basking in the Indian summer!!!

Your slightly bruised cyclist,
Ma Ding

A Roller and a puke green Lamborghini parked outside my Hangzhou apartment.

DECEMBER ALREADY! – 5th December 2011

Where did the autumn go? It seems that I have only just returned to China and in two and a bit weeks I'll be back for Christmas (hooray!!). Talking of Christmas, 1st of December, and all the big stores, shopping malls and hotels have been decorated with the most gaudy bangles and tinsel to welcome the festive season; well, the opportunity for lots more sales really. Nothing is worse than going into a Chinese food shop to buy some fruit and veg, as I did this weekend, to be confronted by the continuous noise of Rudolph the bloody Red-Nosed Reindeer sung with a Chinese/American accent and the checkout assistants wearing the red Santa outfits looking as miserable as sin. There is no religious significance out here, it's just a marketing gimmick and any sense of fun seems to have been completely lost. It won't be long and they'll be re-decorating for Chinese New Year, wearing bright silk clothes and letting off mountains of fireworks, at least there's some cultural relevance!!!!

'Twas my birthday a couple of weeks ago (the paragraph above makes me sound like an old git) and coincidently it was also Steve's (the General Manager) birthday on the same day. Now at the company we have a tradition of giving every employee a cake for their birthday. This is done on a monthly basis with a small celebration and photographs taken with the bosses as they hand out the cakes. For some reason, 34 out of a total workforce of 160 have birthdays in November, so we had a mountain of cakes, all packed in smart boxes, to hand out. Lots of hand shaking and piccies later, Steve and I eventually gave each other our respective cakes (no, there wasn't enough room for all my candles!!!). A couple of days later when we returned to our apartments the evening before our birthday, we were greeted by a ring on the doorbell, and surprise, surprise, we both received birthday cakes from the apartment management. These were quite large cakes and quite independently we decided to take them to work the next day (our actual birthday) to share amongst the office staff. We gave them to Laura (our assistant) to sort out. Mid-way through the morning I had received a couple of thanks for the cake, so I thought a cup of tea and a piece of cake would go down a treat. Well, you've guessed it, Laura had given it all out, so Steve and I, on our actual birthday, had no cake. (I don't really like it that much cos Chinese cakes are full of fluffy cream and taste of nothing.) Anyway we had some fun making Laura feel guilty for an hour or two.

The other weekend I had to go to Hong Kong yet again to renew my visa. This involves flying to Hong Kong (obviously) then making my way across the border with China near the city of Shenzhen and then catching a flight back to Hangzhou. Normally from Hong Kong airport this has involved one high speed train, 3 metro trains, a walk and plenty of queuing at the border to get out of Hong Kong, more queuing to get into China and finally a one hour coach journey to Shenzhen airport. All in all about three hours if the queues are not too bad. Someone suggested I should investigate the coach service that runs from Hong Kong airport to Shenzhen airport as it should be a lot quicker. Well, I had plenty of time since I landed in HK at 1.30pm and my flight out of Shenzhen wasn't until 8.00pm, so I asked around for the best transport options. It seemed that the 'Limousine Service' at £23 was the best option, leaving every 30 minutes, so I had a little bit of lunch, read my book and bought a ticket for the 3.30pm limo service!!!! The limos in question turned out to be 7 seater Toyota people carriers with greasy drivers wearing grubby white shirts and waistcoats to make it look like they were chauffeurs!! No luck for me, I was the only non-Asian in our vehicle and ended up in the middle row wedged between a 'lardy' and a 'smelly' with my bag on my lap because the luggage area was full up with their suitcases. Not a happy bunny but at least they said it would only take 90 minutes. Well the ride was smooth and we got to the border in under an hour, queued up with all the other limos to get out of Hong Kong, and then got in the next queue for China immigration. This is where it all went wrong. Some immigration soldiers decide to take our vehicle out of the queue and put us in another area behind one other similar vehicle. Clearly we were going to be fully searched. The car in front was called forward into a separate bay and we lost sight of it. Then we waited!!!! For about an hour we just sat getting very hot and frustrated, my mind started wandering; is there anything I could be detained for? (nothing I hope), will they use rubber gloves? etc. etc. We were eventually called forward, told to get out of the vehicle with our luggage and sent to a separate room. Our cases were then put through scanners and searched. I only had a small bag just in case the flight was delayed so no problem. In reality it only took about 15 minutes to do the search and luckily no nasty stuff!!! Then we were on our way at 100 miles an hour so that two of the other passengers could maybe catch their 7.00pm flights. Scary, but we got to the airport in about 20 minutes. Perhaps the slow way is the best for next time.

Did you catch the tragic news about the school bus that crashed near Shanghai in which 18 school children were killed? Very tragic and there has been a lot of follow up news concerning overcrowding of transport. This small minibus was actually registered to carry 9 seated passengers but in this case there were 62 people, yes 62, mainly children, crammed in. Because of the traffic congestion I see over-crowded buses every day, I've even taken them myself when there are no taxis.

On Sunday I visited the local Natural History museum. It is all part of a very impressive new complex housing a Science & Technology Museum, a local City Museum and an Art Gallery, built less than 3 years ago next to the Grand Canal and with plenty of small parks and trees surrounding it. The Natural History museum was very educational, well presented and even had some signs in English. Lots of families taking little Zhongy or Lilly to see the dinosaurs etc. Interesting, although not a surprise was the museum shop (another selling opportunity) where apart from the plastic animals, snakes and butterflies was a mineral and stone exhibition where you could buy samples of crystals and minerals. And guess what was there ... yes, for the first time outside of my old place of work in Southern China I found exhibited and for sale my 'Chinese Fortune Stones'. Those of you who were 'wise' enough to buy a stone or two from me will be pleased to know that the Chinese price for an equivalent stone is now about three times what you paid two years ago. Now that's what I call a good investment! Better than the stock markets around the world.

Back to work now to try to make the profit target for December.

Wishing you all the best,
Ma Ding

Yes, it's a Christmas Bunny to cheer us all up!

OH IT'S SO COLD! – 11th January 2012

Following an enjoyable but busy trip home I have returned to China at a time of bitterly cold weather. I don't know why, but the Chinese cold for the same temperature feels much colder and seems to penetrate through the whole body. Hot soup for lunch is the order of the day, but if I have to spend any length of time in the factory the inner warmth quickly disappears. Even the offices are cold and most people are wearing big skiing jacket type things all the time. Shiny black plastic padded jackets are all the rage out here at the moment, although to me it looks as though people are wearing a black bin liner. There's no accounting for taste although as my family tell me I've no sense of fashion.

Translation of signs from Chinese into the equivalent English is a continuous source of amusement. Recently a lot of new road signs have appeared to improve road safety. The best examples that I pass every day on the journey to work are: 'Buckly Up', 'Dont Drive Tiredly' and 'No Drunk Drive'. These signs obviously have the writing in Chinese and an appropriate picture of a seat belt etc. The other one that amused me recently when I was in Shanghai is a new bank called the Wooribank, which is very apt name at this time of financial difficulties. I have taken photos of many other examples of shop and street signs to keep the memories. I'm sure that if we Brits were to ever write Chinese on our road signs and shops we would make a complete mess of it and the Chinese would be laughing at our incompetence. At least they make the effort.

As one of very few westerners in a strange land there is an unwritten common bond, so when you are walking around and pass another western looking foreigner you usually give a knowing nod to each other as if to say 'we are one of the few'. This does not happen in places like Shanghai where there are so many westerners they all ignore each other as if they were in London. So, the other day I was walking to the bread shop and I noticed in the crowd of black hair and Chinese faces a short, tubby, balding grey-haired westerner (no it was not a mirror!!!!) and as he came towards me our eyes met, we said hello and he stopped to talk. We exchanged the normal pleasantries and he told me what he was up to. It turns out he is a Canadian physician, working for the World Health Organisation, assigned to the main hospital in Hangzhou. His specialism is bird flu and he was telling me of a recent outbreak in the UK (of which I've heard nothing) and the potential spread from Hong Kong. He felt that at the moment the problem was contained but his exact words were (say it in an American accent) "if the bird flu gets to Mainland China you'd better put your head between your legs an' kiss your ass goodbye". On that cheery note I wished him luck and bade him farewell thinking what other potential nasties are our governments keeping from us?

In a similar vein there has been a rash of food quality issues in China recently. Perhaps they have always been there but now that there is more openness in reporting and the government is trying hard to promote Chinese quality they are coming down hard on the offenders. The latest concerns the death of a 10 year old with two others still in a coma after drinking something called 'Pulpy Super Milky'. I think I would be put off by the name Pulpy Super Milky itself. We wait with interest to see how this plays out and who (if anyone) is responsible. Last year the Chief Executive of a Chinese company, producing milk products for babies where harmful additives caused the death of several children, was executed.

The Christmas decorations have all come down and have been replaced by thousands of red Chinese lanterns in readiness for the Chinese New Year. The shop assistants have swapped their red and white Santa hats for bright silk waist-coats, however they're still all as miserable as sin!!! The shops are stacked out with presentation boxes of baijiu (the really nasty local spirit drink) and everybody seems to be buying like mad for what is only three official days of holiday; having said that many people will travel hundreds of miles to get home and so the general holiday period is closer to a week. We will have our company party this Friday and unfortunately as the boss I will be expected to toast all 154 employees individually. Hopefully I can do it a table at a time (18 tables) and so limit the consumption; whatever, it's going to be a tough test for my constitution!!! I'll let you know how I get on.

The big UK bosses visited this week and they've started interviewing for my replacement so we will see if there is someone good enough (ha ha!!) who will hopefully not have to work too much notice and can start soon. The target is to get back home to enjoy the late spring and summer when I am assured that we will have wonderful weather (I wish). However I definitely will not have to see what I'm breathing.

Happy New Year and I hope you are still sticking to your New Year resolutions (mine is no choccy during work days – a real tough one).

Ma Ding

I think the marketing message for these clothes has been lost
in translation.

One of my favourite drinking establishments ... Yummy!!!

FIREWORKS AND YET MORE FIREWORKS –
2nd February 2012

So Chinese New Year has been and gone with only four employees deciding they didn't want to come back to work in Hangzhou and will stay with their families, probably until the money runs out and then they'll be back for a job. Although I have been in China for about three Chinese New Year celebrations I have never seen or heard so many fireworks. Certainly the major display on the actual New Year's day was as spectacular as ever, but on the days leading up and for over a week after there have been loads of fireworks, some interesting to watch and others just annoying. Most businesses and lots of families will let off some fireworks at various times to ward off the evil spirits as we head into the year of the Dragon. But walking down the street only to find someone lets off a multiple firecracker just behind you is no fun, they are really very loud! It could be that they think I'm an evil big nose spirit; well they have certainly put me off. And the timing, from 6 in the morning until around midnight (I was even woken up by some antisocial local letting off a major firecracker at 3 in the morning); it just feels constant for nearly two weeks. Even our factory, on the first day back at work, let off several very noisy fireworks close to my office window. I thought we were being attacked!! Roll on November the 5th!!!

So we had our Company New Year party a couple of weeks ago with many employees doing odd performances, dances, sketches and songs. If I'm honest they weren't that good but everyone got into the swing of it and Steve and I had to get up on stage and do some 'Guess that Tune' thing. Apparently there is some popular Chinese TV show where contestants put headphones on and hum along to a Chinese song which the panel has to guess. Well Steve and I found it very difficult, it's virtually impossible to sing or hum an unknown Chinese tune at the same time as it's being played to you through headphones. We eventually got a couple right, mainly by luck I think. Anyway it was a good laugh (for the workers). There then followed a raffle with some unusually good prizes which apart from the bottles of cooking oil also included duvets, with a washing machine as the major prize. I have to say the catering left a lot to be desired (the food was crap) and although there was a bottle of firewater (baijiu) on each table Steve and I stuck to the local fizzy beer. We obviously had to go round toasting the 160 employees but did it by table, so only 16 large glasses of fizzy beer plus various individual employees who wanted to have a drink and photo with the big foreign bosses. We made our excuses whilst we were still standing (but feeling very bloated) and left them all to it. The next day, however, there had obviously been a little bit of a problem with our Maintenance Manager provoking some of the employees from another province because he started receiving death threats. A bit dramatic but he was really scared and we had to get them all together and make them realise it was just the drink talking. It appears to have settled down.

I had to go down to Guangzhou (formerly known as Canton) on the South coast of China to discuss a contract with a new Sales Manager who is based in the city. He lives near the harbour area and when he asked me if I liked eating seafood, because I said yes he decided to take me to one of the 'best value places'. Well this turned out to be a huge covered market area selling anything and everything that's ever come from the sea. We entered and were followed around by some woman who I was told would help us with the cooking. The sales guy chose some strange shellfish things and a large sea urchin, I played safe and picked a long squid thing. Everything we looked at was supposedly 'hao chi' (delicious) although I have to say you really did wonder whether it was something even a dog would eat!! We then had to choose some veg and followed this woman out of a back door and down a narrow street which had lots of little eating places (restaurant is the wrong word, in fact canteen is too good a word). We entered one of these 'establishments' the size of a double-length garage and all our purchases were handed to someone who showed us where to sit, then disappeared out the back to do the cooking. I did get a large bottle of cold beer. Just as well because I found myself at a rickety old wooden table looking out across the narrow road to what can only be described as an open slaughter-house. These two old ladies in overalls and big blue wellies were virtually continuously killing, boiling, plucking and chopping up hens, ducks and geese, probably about 20 in the time I was eating my food, which I have to say was quite tasty. It cost £7 for the cooking service and the beer, but I didn't get a discount for the entertainment!!!!

Another quick meal story ... I promised to take Kerry, my Chinese teacher out for a meal after my lesson on the Thursday before New Year. Because it was raining heavily we decided to go somewhere near and chose a restaurant just across the road which Steve and I had thought we might try out some time. We entered downstairs where there were some fish tanks and a big board with pictures displaying the many different dishes. A waitress was there to help us choose and take our order before we went upstairs to get a table. No problem as we chose a pork dish, some vegetables and a fish dish plus my cold beer. So we went upstairs, sat down and waited. After 10 minutes I wondered where my cold beer was so we summoned a waiter and he told us that they have no cold beer; well, put some ice around a bottle for 5 minutes, I suggested; they have no ice! I don't like warm lager so I said forget it. The vegetables arrived, so we tucked in, then 10 minutes later the pork dish arrived, however there seemed to be very little pork meat in it, only fat!! We waited expectantly for the fish but it didn't arrive so we called the waiter and they admitted they'd forgotten it. So we asked to see the manager, he also took ages to arrive. He did apologise and said that if we waited another 10 minutes the fish would be with us. I then used my best Chinese to tell him that as there was no cold beer, no meat on the pork and no fish, I had no money. We left without paying!!

Now is the footbath season again. Every supermarket is selling loads of these things and as you walk in the entrance you have to find a way through various stalls of these things promoting different brands. People get the chance to try them out, taking off their smelly socks and sitting down with their feet in hot bubbly water whilst the assistant extols the virtues of wet feet!! The good part of this season is the very delicious (I mean it this time) small oranges called 'jinju' and lychees, not the canned variety we get in the UK, but freshly picked ready for peeling, luffly!!! I often try to check what ingredients are in some of the packet foods I buy and the other day I was buying some stuff to make up my own breakfast cereal (what a sad git!) and I picked up a packet of sunflower seeds. Turning the pack over the list of ingredients just happened to be in both Chinese and English . . . and these sunflower seeds were made from '100% melon pips'!!!!

Best wishes to you all during this cold patch.
Ma Ding

I couldn't even begin to describe what this food is. However I'm sure it's extremely tasty!!!

Urchin squidge served in an urchin!

PAROLE DATE SET – 5th March 2012

At long last I've got a date for my parole. I go before the parole board on the 15th March and hopefully if nothing goes wrong I should be out on parole, with good behaviour obviously, by the first week in June. I had hoped to be out earlier but the Governor has taken a long time to get new staff and I'll probably have to leave my cell to the new inmate. With this delay I've managed to get a week's compassionate home leave during the last week of March, but they are providing me with an ankle tag so I can't disappear!! So home for early summer and nothing planned so I'll try and steer clear of any 'job' offers for several months and get used to life on the outside!! (And you all thought I was working in China.)

The Buick 7 seater company car that takes us to work and back every day desperately needed replacing. It's done 293,000 km and the way Munki drives it the steering and brakes are regularly protesting with strange groaning noises. The car previously belonged to the Shanghai office of our parent company so it has a Shanghai number plate. This was a bit of luck since, whilst the car has been steadily depreciating over the last 4 years, the value of the number plate has been going up. So much so that the car itself was valued at £4,000 but the Shanghai number plate was valued at £5,500!!! No, it's not a clever combination of letters and numbers that spells 'Dwagon' or 'Flied Wice', it is all to do with the way that car usage is being restricted in the big Chinese cities. Basically if you buy a new car, you then have to go to a number plate auction and there are only so many number plates available to buy every month. Supply and demand takes over, so whereas in our city, Hangzhou, the average cost of a number plate is about £500, in Shanghai it is ten times that. So we made a nice little profit on the sale of the old banger and have replaced it with another similar vehicle which Munki is very quickly wearing out.

As I've mentioned before, Hangzhou is a very ancient and famous city built on the side of a small lake called West Lake.

It really is one of the top tourist destinations in China and the lakeside is usually full of groups following the guide (who holds up a flag) walking around the famous buildings, temples and pagodas. There is also music playing in many areas and as I was walking around the lake the other weekend I noticed that for all its Chinese history a lot of western music was being played over the speaker systems. For example, in one location, every hour there is a very spectacular water fountain display with coloured lights and music; several rows of seats are available for visitors to sit and take in this 15 minute show. Although I've walked past several times before and been impressed with the display, the other weekend my legs were feeling particularly weary so I sat down to watch the full display. The final two pieces of music were Jupiter from the Planets Suite (Holst), used more recently as the theme for the Rugby World Cup, and the William Tell Overture, or the theme from the Lone Ranger as I would call it (I couldn't see Tonto anywhere). Then as I walked home across one of the causeways they were playing the Skye Boat Song on the speakers (the Scots get everywhere, don't they??). So although the Chinese are taking over the world, they are adopting some of our more cultured aspects to go alongside their spitting!!

Another regular point of interest for the tourists around West Lake is a couple of large trees where there always seem to be squirrels running around. The Chinese seem fascinated by these animals and although rats and similar animals are eaten out here, the bushy tails (the squirrels, not the Chinese) make a big difference, so out come the cameras and some locals are even selling squirrel food at 20p a bag.

As with most large western companies there is an annual bonus scheme which usually pays out something in February or March following the previous year's results. Bridon is no different and although the business here in Hangzhou didn't have a good 2011 the Bridon Group did OK. The bonus scheme is structured so that the employees feel part of the big family and get some bonus based on the Regional (Asia in our case) and the Worldwide results. Well this is all calculated by the big central computer and I received the list of bonus payments for all my people. For some reason the guys who operate the machines get nothing whereas the maintenance and inspection workers get something, these people work side by side so this was going to cause problems. Secondly when I looked in detail at the payments some of the people were getting a bonus (for the year) of £3.50 before stoppages (less than 2 hours' pay), in fact most people were getting less than £10. With the big bosses probably getting tens of thousands of pounds this did not seem fair. Anyway one of the benefits of being independent (and not being part of the bonus scheme) is that I can speak my mind (ever so subtly, you know me!!!). So in the cause of fairness I have ensured that all of my employees will receive something and there will be a minimum payment of £20. It probably won't be appreciated but at least it won't cause a lot of internal strife.

Lots of visitors coming in the next few weeks, even the Senior Executive team are having their Board meeting here in two weeks' time. For some reason our business has improved since I've been here so they all want to take some credit and help!!!!

I hope to see some of you at the end of March when I'm back for a week. In the meantime enjoy the sunshine (you must have it 'cos it's not here!!).

Best wishes,
Ma Ding

Dancing in the street. Mainly women but often ballroom dancing for couples in the mornings.

SPRING TIME IN CHINA – 25th April 2012

Last Saturday was a fine day but with a very strong wind. I did venture out on my bike but it was a bit precarious at times with other road users swaying about all over the place. The good news about the wind is that it tends to clear the air so that by Sunday with only a gentle breeze and the temperatures in the high 20s (about 75°F) it was probably the best day weather-wise I have experienced in Hangzhou. I decided to go to a hill park called Wushan Park overlooking the West Lake, which I've been meaning to get to for several weeks now, but only on a clear day when the views should be great. It certainly is a very natural park built on one of the higher hills next to the lake, lots of large green trees and plenty of flowers. At the summit of the hill stands a big square pagoda which I climbed to get above the tree line and see the views. At the top of about 20 flights of stairs I discovered not only a 360 degree balcony, but also in the centre of it all a small restaurant in which a group of locals were obviously having a bit of a party, lots of shouting and some singing. This at about 11.30 in the morning, but the Chinese often have a Sunday brunch at which lots of alcohol is consumed. Oh well, each to their own, but I wouldn't have liked to get down the stairs in the state some of them were in!!! Anyway the views should have been wonderful but ... In England, on a clear day we can see for miles; in China, on what you think is a clear day, it's still misty. So the mountains on the other side of the lake about 5 miles away were certainly visible but in a misty, foggy way, or was it my eyes losing capability after the stair climb? I honestly think that China just has a general haze in most areas.

We've had our new company car now for just over 4 weeks and Munki (our driver) had his first crash (that I know about!) last week. Just a normal bump with both parties claiming it was the other's fault. The insurance companies will fight to decide. However I have really begun to notice both an increase in the traffic and with it, more aggressive driving. When I first arrived here it would take about 30 minutes to get to work in the morning and about 40 minutes getting back in the evening. No particular hold ups apart from lots of traffic lights. Well in the last few weeks it has taken about 5 to 10 minutes longer each way with some traffic jams on the 5 lane expressway as a result of too much traffic. They estimate about 2000 new cars are coming onto the Hangzhou roads every week so before long it will become gridlocked. Having been working in different places in China I now have a theory as to the stages of a city's driving culture development. Firstly it all starts (as Liuzhou in 2007) as a bit of a free-for-all, lots of pedestrians, bikes, trikes, motorbikes, cars, trucks and buses going about their business, not too worried about the rules of the road because there's enough space and everybody is pretty cautious as to what is around them. Also they are generally able to get to where they are going in a reasonable time. The second phase, and I think this is where Hangzhou's at, is whilst drivers still don't follow the rules (red lights meaning stop, not maybe; drive on the right, not any direction that's convenient, etc.) the build up of traffic means that if people don't follow the rules hold ups get worse and many more accidents happen. This gets drivers more annoyed, they then become more aggressive and even more accidents happen. Last Thursday driving back home we saw 4 separate accidents and then on Friday morning there was a 'classic' between 2 electric bikes at a crossroads. We had stopped and had a clear view of the accident as it happened; obviously one bike had decided to go through the lights when they had just turned red and from 90 degrees another had decided to get going early before his light had turned green. Well they both collided in the centre and it took a while for both to get up and start shouting at each other. This situation then created a mini roundabout in the middle of the crossroad with again lots of hooting and annoyed drivers fighting their way forward (now I know why it's called a 'cross road'!!!!). The next development stage is a bit like Beijing where drivers have now started to follow the rules but there are just far too many vehicles on the roads so it all comes to a grinding halt several times a day. Maybe the final phase is everyone goes back to having an allotment in the country and riding horses? Now there's progress for you!!! I will be pleased to come home to the relatively civilised driving experience of the UK. Hangzhou has now introduced driving restrictions during peak times. This is all based on the final digit on the number plate. We have a zero on our company vehicle so now on a Friday we have to get out of the city centre before 7.00am and return to the apartment either before 4.30pm or after 7.00pm (so early finish on Fridays . . . hooray!).

There are some good things about China but occasionally when they come together it causes a problem. As I think I've told you before the pavements nearly all have a central ribbed area, usually a different colour, so that partially sighted or blind people can feel their way along more easily. Also lots and lots of older people take part in exercises in the early morning or evening and there are many small parks with simple exercise machines for them to use, or they do ballroom dancing, or aerobics. This is all so that they keep the doctor (and the costs) away. The other evening as I was out on my walk (yes, an old man doing his exercise!!!) I noticed a little old lady walking backwards (apparently walking backwards uses other muscles) towards me, clapping her hands and occasionally hitting her shoulders (why oh why oh why??). Now she was trying to be clever and by feeling/following the ribbed portion of the pavement she didn't have to look behind her.

Unfortunately I couldn't stop her as she walked backwards into a bucket of restaurant slops left in the middle of the pavement outside a small eating place; she was not happy as she picked herself up, shouted lots of obscenities and tried to wipe the old food from her trousers. Sometimes it just doesn't pay to be too smart!!! I will continue to walk forwards where I can see all the problems and try to avoid them.

Another cultural note is that as you have probably heard the Chinese like to drink wine and as with lots of things they like to show off by buying and drinking 'good western stuff'. So last year China imported 50,000 bottles of Chateau

Lafitte Rothschild from France (you've probably got a case or two in your cellar!!!). Well the other part of the statistic is that China consumed 2 million bottles of this very same wine last year. Take a bottle of Red Dragon plonk, slap on a fancy French label and sell for £100 per bottle, a great little business!!! As with DVDs, watches and designer bags the government is trying to crack down, so get your orders in quickly.

I hope you are all getting prepared for the Jubilee parties, I'll probably be home in time for some leftover cake!!

Best wishes
Ma Ding

Yet another minor accident. Luckily no one hurt this time.

Please note the ribbed stones as an aid for blind people, cleverly avoiding the tree. A great place to park the bike!!!

SCARY – 14th May 2012

Scary!!! I was woken up early on Saturday morning by the sound of what I can only describe as air-raid sirens. Now Saturday morning is the day I usually get up later, at about 8.00am because Friday is a very early start (up at 5.45am for a 6.30am departure to the factory) due to car number plate restrictions. The noise lasted for about 10 minutes and stopped so I got up and made myself a cup of tea, but then the sirens started up again and were really deafening. I was beginning to get a bit worried because I know the Chinese are having a bit of a military stand-off with the Vietnamese and Philippines but I didn't expect Hangzhou to be affected. The sirens would die down after 10 minutes but then start up again. I switched on the TV and turned to Chinese news and saw some 'live' pictures of what seemed to be a chemical plant on fire with smoke and flames billowing from it, lots of fire engines, soldiers and people in silver chemical suits running around. One of the large chemical storage towers then exploded. The sirens continued so I went down to reception to ask what was going on. Apparently (and I should really have known this because I was in China at the time) it was the 4th anniversary of the Sichuan earthquake in 2008 that killed about 80,000 people. As I've mentioned before the Chinese commemorate events such as these and funerals with as much noise as they can for as long as they can, compared to our minute of silence. I was relieved and the chemical plant fire was one part of a live practice in the event of another earthquake, televised to give the populace confidence that the authorities are better prepared now.

Last week I had a bit of a Mr Bean experience. This is the season of mosquitoes, not that they have affected me elsewhere in China, and so the stores are selling lots of anti-mozzy stuff. One of the items that I've seen before and has intrigued me is what can only be described as a tennis racket (maybe a little smaller) which obviously has electrified 'strings' for swatting the insects. As you know in Painswick we often have lots of wasps and flies during the summer, so I thought I would buy one of these things that varied in price from about £3 for a standard model up to £8 for a super-dooper rechargeable version. They were hanging on racks in clear plastic covers. So I picked one off the rack and proceeded to take it out of the cover, did a little bit of a Roger Federer impression, by which time some of the locals were looking my way. I touched the 'strings' to check how it worked and got a real big jolt of an electric shock, let out a loud 'arhh' and dropped the thing causing bits to break off the handle. It was similar to the shock you get (if you are stupid enough to try!!) when you touch a cattle wire. I recovered quickly, picked it up carefully, shoved it back in the plastic cover, kicked the plastic chips on the floor under the racking, put it back roughly where it had come from and promptly rushed off to the vegetable section, ignoring the onlookers. I think I'll wait a week or two before deciding to buy this dangerous item, although I am still tempted.

It's also the season of pineapple, mango and snails. So I've always got some fresh pineapple and mango in my cooking now, on my cereal in the morning, with my salad at lunchtime (yes, I've gone a bit healthy eating at the moment) and with my ice cream in the evenings (so not that healthy!!). However the snails I am happy to pass on, although I have eaten both French and Chinese snails in the past, and it has to be said that I prefer the French variety since they are fatter and usually covered in garlic sauce, whereas the Chinese snails are long, thin and curly. The Chinese name for them is 'lousi', pretty close to an apt English word I think!!! The Chinese, as ever, have a saying for the occasion ... this being 'lousi at Qingming is more nutritious than goose'. So now you know!!!

Talking of food, there are regular food scares in China and so with the London Olympics approaching fast the Chinese Olympic team have only been allowed to eat fully inspected food, their diets being monitored very carefully. There's probably a whole new team of Olympic food tasters getting fatter by the day!! In fact the Chinese government has introduced a reward scheme for anyone who gives a tip-off of a potential food problem. The reward is Rmb200 (about £20). I really don't know where to start with my list but I can see me having a very lucrative new career being paid for all the suspect food and drink that I've experienced in the last few years.

Well, less than 4 weeks to go now and I'm really looking forward to getting back (in spite of the list of jobs to do!!!).

Best wishes
Ma Ding

The latest summer wear seen around Hangzhou West Lake. Nice!!

小草害羞笑 请君勿打扰
Grass Is Shy And Smiling
Please No Disturbing

A slightly more subtle 'Keep off the Grass' sign than we have in the UK.

THE LAST POST – May 30th 2012

Well I'm now counting down with only a few more days to go and although this has been a really good assignment I'm looking forward to getting back home. There's only so much pollution, dangerous traffic, dodgy food and spitting I can take at a time. However it has to be said that I have enjoyed this assignment more than most: generally the company culture has been easy to adjust to, we've managed to significantly improve the business, Hangzhou is one of the best places to live in China and not forgetting, I've been well paid for 10 months!!!

Even though Hangzhou has many foreigners living in the city there are places where a 'big nose' is not a common sight, and having my own bicycle I did go off exploring at weekends and would end up in some strange parts of the city. Last weekend for example I got nearly as far as the river (with the famous tidal bore) and due to a sore bum (narrow bicycle seat and lardy arse!!) decided to park the bike and walk for a bit. As ever, lots of people about, but no foreigners. Anyway this family, Mum, Dad and a little girl holding Daddy's hand, were walking towards me and as we passed the little girl's head turned round to gawk at me. I turned to look just in time to see her walk straight into a bus stop, banging her head. She obviously started to cry and her Mum and Dad tried to comfort her as he looked at me with daggers and shouted at me as if it was all my fault. I carried on walking feeling a bit guilty, knowing that at my ripe old age I can still turn heads, but not really for the right reasons!!!

As you know many parts of Asia are well known for all the copies and fake products that can be found in various markets, particularly DVDs, famous brand watches and lots of western brand clothes and bags. So I was reading in the paper the other day that producing fake items has taken another twist. In the same way that we might have some nuts or cheese straws as nibbles before a meal the Chinese would delight in chewing on a chicken's foot or a pig's ear. I have in fact eaten both items early on in my time in China and I can

178

honestly say that you are not missing much. Well the latest food scandal is the sale of fake pigs' ears. These are made of gelatine with various chemicals to ensure they have the right colour, taste and texture. Anyway the article in the paper suggested that many millions of these fake pigs' ears were currently in circulation and the expert (a pig's ear expert???) was asked how to spot the genuine one from the fake. This is what he said ... "you will find that the real pig's ear has several hairs and if you look closely there will be small blood vessels visible"!!!! Makes the real thing so much more appetising, doesn't it???? Would the collective noun for a lot of pigs' ears be a herd???

As in many countries, inflation has made the small coins less and less valuable in terms of their ability to buy anything. The smallest common coin is called a mao (rhymes with cow) and is the size of a penny but silver in colour. At current exchange rates it is roughly equivalent to one penny. So since I don't like carrying loads of these around, after I return from shopping I drop them into a bowl together with the paper bank note equivalent of 5p which is called a jiao (also like cow). So after several months in China I have now got a bowlful of maos and jiaos, and I am not taking them back home with me. On Sunday I put them all in a small plastic bag and carried them with me when I went out walking, knowing that at some stage I would pass a beggar on the streets and I would hopefully make their day. Near the main shopping area I saw a middle aged lady sitting at the side of the road begging, however she didn't look to be too incapable of work so I carried on. I then passed an old man who looked very bedraggled and so I stopped a few paces beyond him, got my bag of coins out and went back. He didn't look up as I dropped the bag into his begging bowl and I wished him a good weekend in my best Chinese. As I walked away he suddenly realised what was in the bag and shouted after me, thanking me in some strange local dialect for my generosity. I'm sure he was thanking me due to his big toothless grin, or he could have been saying "What the hell am I going to do with all these little coins?" Unfortunately everyone began to stare at me and I was concerned that I would suddenly be the target for a lot more potential beggars. I quickly walked away, my good deed done and knowing that the beggar was probably going off with his newfound fortune (about £5) to buy some fake pigs' ears for his tea!!!

That's about it for now. The new Managing Director is starting to get involved and I will move out of my office at the end of the week. Then a few more days trying to finalise May results and no doubt a farewell banquet where I will be required to drink the dreaded baijiu (powerful rice spirit), toasting with all the managers until I can't stand up.

Best wishes to you all and I look forward to seeing you during the summer.

Ma Ding

The Bridon Hangzhou management team.

SOME LOOSE ENDS

From the middle of May the city of Hangzhou was adorned with posters trying to make the citizens more conscientious and probably improve Hangzhou as a holiday destination for western tourists. In fact Amy noticed an advert for Hangzhou on a London bus recently.

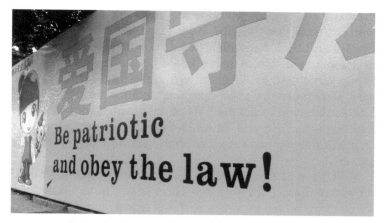

Various large posters all around the city of Hangzhou.

The Wedding Invitation. You may remember that very early on I went to visit the pandas in Chengdu and a guy called Brian Li acted as my guide and translator. Well, Brian eventually came to work for us in Liuzhou as a Sales Engineer and over the years has been promoted to Sales Manager; we have kept in touch. He invited me as a 'special guest' to his wedding and luckily I was able to find the time to attend, knowing that to have a 'big nose' at his wedding would lend it some kudos in the eyes of his in-laws. So I turned up at the wedding celebration where about 300 guests would attend and was immediately asked to be photographed with the bride and groom outside the venue as guests were arriving. Brian then told me that he would like me to say a few words during the formal part of the evening and could I go and see Shelly, the Master of Ceremonies, who would tell me what I was expected to say.

I found Shelly who seemed to be rushing around with lots of pieces of paper but she stopped and handed me some form of script in both Chinese and English. Then she proceeded to explain my role: "After the bride and groom enter the hall and get up onto the stage, Brian will firstly say a few words of welcome and thanks, then I will invite you to

183

the stage and explain who you are. I will ask you to come up with 3 words that describe Brian. It's OK, you can do it in English and I will translate. Then as you were responsible for bringing him to the city and you are his mentor I will ask you to say something to wish him well in the future with his new wife, after which you will take the wedding vows." What?? Yes, I was going to act the part of the vicar or ship's captain and do the . . . "Do you, Brian Li, take this woman to be your wedded wife, to have and to hold, from this day forth" . . . etc. etc.

Well this was a new one on me, and I've mentioned many times that there's always a new surprise in China. So, always ready to try a new experience, this is exactly what happened about 30 minutes later, much to the delight of everyone in the room. I must point out that Brian and his wife were legally married during a small civil ceremony the previous week so my performance was really only for show. However this may provide a new career opportunity when other work finally dries up.

The Captain taking the wedding vows.

184

Travel: During the last few years I have been lucky enough to visit many well-known and not so well-known sites in China. From sacred mountains to ancient cities and in June 2012 to Jiuzhaigou, one of the most beautiful places I have ever been to in the world. Often I have been the only foreigner, having joined a typical Chinese tour, and have always found the local tourists eager to help me understand what's going on. They are usually amused and impressed that I manage to speak some of their language which helps every time.

I have also been constantly amused by the poor translation of Chinese notices and shop signs into English. There really has to be a great job for a translator who expresses the meaning of the Chinese words and not just the direct translation of each word.

I finish this section with some additional photographs which I hope you find interesting.

The ever popular 'Empty Club' near my Wuxi apartment.

Did they expect us to run out of this Nanjing tourist site?

Is this where the phrase 'I don't give a monkey's' comes from?

As a 'big nose' I could go here for a trendy improvement!

A subtly titled club for those who want to show their success.

Spend lots of money here to make the owner happy.

The scenic Huangshan (Yellow Mountain) area.

Lao Ma (Old Horse) with his namesake bush.

Silver Cave in Guangxi Province.

189

Sunset over the Karst mountains around Yangshuo.

The author walks the Great Wall of China.

The truly wonderful scenery of Jiuzhaigou in Sichuan province.

191

The Fifth Session

Chengdu, Sichuan Province

BACK IN CHINA – 4th November 2013

Here beginneth the fifth session.

Well, this time I'm in the west of China, in a city called Chengdu in Sichuan province, where the pandas come from. I'm working for a small UK engineering plc which has had a presence in China since 2010 and wants to expand rapidly. As the General Manager of the Chinese business, I am in charge of a small facility with about 20 people which is situated inside the customer's factory. This customer (a Chinese/US joint venture) manufactures MRI scanners and we provide all the pressure vessels. (I won't bore you with the techy stuff now). Now another major customer wants us to produce the same sort of parts to supply to their Chinese factory in the south of China, so we are well on the way to having another much larger factory up and running by March next year. This new factory is about 5 miles away from the first one.

So, I've been learning about all the issues that the previous GM left behind and getting to know the team as well as key people from our customers and suppliers. Not only that but I've been trying to find an apartment so that I don't have to live out of a suitcase in an expensive hotel. Busy, busy, busy!

Thursday before last I went out with one of our people to look at apartments. The current Production Manager, Michael, a Brit from Wolverhampton who has been in China for several years, lives near the city centre and we share the driver to get to work and back. Therefore my search area for apartments was pretty limited. In the space of about 6 hours, with lots of hanging about, I managed to see 8 apartments in 3 different complexes. Nothing was ideal . . . great apartments at reasonable prices but next to the main street in the city, so a constant drone of traffic, hooting and shouting. I quickly discounted other apartments in that block. Next came a complex called the Europa, but both apartments were dark with very antique-type furnishings fit for King George the Third. The last apartment complex, called Utopia (hardly),

194

offered a couple of options which seemed reasonable, so understanding that I had to compromise, I plumped for something that offered the space and light, but I have to say that the furniture is much too ornate for my simple tastes. We did the deal and I moved in last Saturday.

But, although the furniture is in place, plus TV, microwave etc. I still had to rapidly get bedding, towels, cutlery, plates, glasses, cookware and numerous other items without even getting to cleaning products, food, beer and wine. So all weekend I was going back and forth to various supermarkets to get the stuff. The security guard was most amused as just about every couple of hours throughout the weekend I would walk through the barrier laden with all sorts of stuff. My aim was to be in a position to cook a Sunday roast and settle down for rest sometime on Sunday afternoon. The biggest problem was finding a shop that sold potatoes, eventually found in a smallish store about a mile from my apartment. And yes, I did manage to cook roast pork with roast pots and veg, topped with Bisto gravy (brought from the UK), washed down with a bottle of red wine and quickly followed by a snooze.

The highlight (or lowlight) of the weekend was my trip to IKEA. What a nightmare. You probably remember from previous emails or my book that driving in China is a challenge, with many people going in the wrong direction or just stopping in the middle of the road, etc. Well if you have ever done an IKEA shop you will know that the store is laid out so that you must follow the floor arrows from entrance to check-outs, passing by all the sections. Well, that Chinese trolley driving is exactly the same as that on the road, but this time 'trolley rage' takes over, with several bruised toes and crunches. After not many minutes I had reached the end of my tolerance and needed to get out, but couldn't ... I eventually got spewed out of the IKEA sausage machine feeling very worn out. I'll not go there again!

Best wishes to you all,

Ma Ding

ONE MONTH GONE – 21st November 2013

With only 2 weeks in the new job my UK boss announced that he was leaving, also the 'main man' in our only Chinese customer, a Brit, announced that he is being 'moved'. So I really have had an immediate effect on the business, but not in the way I hoped. I think it has to be said that the previous UK boss and this Brit working for the Chinese customer had kept most of the business dealings between themselves which bred quite a lot of ill-feeling within the Chinese customer's management team. So I'm rapidly trying to build bridges and understand the complex financial situation that has been set up between this Chinese customer, my Chinese business and the UK-based business, with purchase orders, delivery notes and invoices going every which way.

My new boss is an ex-David Brown person (I worked for David Brown during my 3rd session in China) so although he worked for a different UK division to me, he knows many of the people I worked with at that time. He should be visiting in early December so we will be able to exchange some interesting stories of persons past.

Further to my last email when I explained the problems of getting in and out of IKEA, I was discussing this with a foreign colleague who said that the IKEA store in Chengdu is one of their most successful in the world, but they had to change the way the store was set up and functioned to appeal to the locals. For instance the toy section is next to the bed section which allows families to have a morning out; the kids play with all the toys whilst the adults have a snooze on the beds. IKEA have to regularly change the sheets, but after a few hours of entertainment the families usually set off around the store and buy stuff.

The Chinese often try to make things look good, but they rarely think it through properly. A couple of examples of this are; firstly the many paved areas around the city, apartments and shopping areas. They always like to have interesting patterns, rather than the same old grey slabs we would often use in the UK. So some bright architect uses a mixture of coloured concrete, stone and marble paving slabs. This is great when the weather is fine but as soon there is the slightest bit of rain the marble becomes just like walking on ice. But since you are walking on alternative grippy stuff and slidy stuff it's all a bit odd if you don't want to fall over. Always looking down with a couple of normal speed steps then small, slow careful paces, Monty Python's Ministry of Silly Walks comes to mind! My work shoes are horrendous for this, but it's fun to see others struggle and either bump into other pedestrians 'cos they are looking down or just fall over anyway.

The second example is that on some of the motorways around Chengdu they decided to make the markings for every kilometre more beautiful. Normally there is just a simple marker in the central reservation with a number on it indicating how many kms from the start of the motorway. Well some other bright spark thought it would look better if as well as the simple marker, four very large and colourful pot plants were put in the central reservation every kilometre. Well last Friday we were driving back home from the factory only to get held up in a traffic jam, oh dear, we thought, another rush hour accident. No, not that, it was the plant watering truck blocking the outside lane as it went diligently for every kilometre stopping to water the plants. To add insult to injury a few minutes after we got past the hold up, it started raining!

I understand that nice Mr Cameron our Prime Minister will be visiting China soon and apparently will visit Chengdu. It could be helpful, but on the other hand …

It's getting slightly colder here now with regular morning mist (or pollution), but only four weeks and I'll be back for Christmas and the clean, crisp and damp Cotswold air!!

Best wishes from the East,
Ma Ding

WINTER RULES – 8th December 2013

Ni Hao,

Winter has now arrived in Chengdu, the temperature has dropped significantly during the last few days and the wind makes it feel really chilly. Even without the change of weather I have been able to deduce that winter will soon be here from items available to buy outside at nearly every crossroads and also in store. All the bigger stores now have stacks of slippers, electric hot water bottles, thermals and furry toilet seat covers. Please let me have your orders and I will bring them home in time for Christmas. What better present for an older relative than a bright orange fluffy toilet seat cover to stop the shock of easing down onto cold plastic?? I have invested in a couple of electric hot water bottles and a cosy blanket in readiness for the dark evenings lying on the couch watching DVDs. I'm not sure how effective my apartment's heating will be and unfortunately there is no possibility of a warming, real log fire. Most heating systems that I've encountered over the years in China are really air-conditioning systems designed to keep the rooms cool during the hot summers, rather than being an effective heating system for the winters.

Last weekend an enterprising chap set up a make-your-own duvet facility outside my apartment block. I'm not sure that this is a real speculative purchase when you are coming home from work in the evening, thinking shall I get in and have some food and a beer or shall I make a new duvet as a surprise present for the wifey? It might be that it appeals to those who want a thicker duvet, or double duvets for the winter nights.

In my wanderings last weekend, I came across an older style Chinese supermarket called Trust Mart. Now I know that in other cities these stores have been taken over by Walmart (owners of Asda) and re-branded as such. Obviously, the re-branding exercise hasn't reached Chengdu yet. Any way I did discover that this store was significantly cheaper that Carrefour (although not as convenient) and the Chilean red wine was a real bargain at between 4 and 7 pounds a bottle. So I have now stocked up and have enough to keep me going for ... days! So maybe when Walmart have got all these stores re-branded I could use the old name ... Trust Mart for my new company selling books and Chinese stones. Or don't you trust Mart?

You may recall that in a previous city I complained (as I do!) about the avenues of trees on the narrow pavements that take up so much width that you have to walk in the gutters. Well Chengdu is different. Lots of tree-lined streets with nice wide pavements so no need to walk in the gutters ... you think. Well, think again, the pavements being nice and wide are now filled with parked cars or with motorcycles and tuk-tuks (motorised 3 wheelers) driving every which way. So it's walking the gutters again for me!!!

You may also remember me telling you the legend behind the dreaded Moon Cake festival, which thank goodness I just missed this year, it being held in early October and me not arriving until the 21st. The Moon Cakes, which are given as gifts to all and sundry, celebrate the Princess Chang'e living for ever on the moon with a jade rabbit ...and the Moon Cakes taste horrible!! Well several years on and the Chinese are just about to send their latest rocket into space, this time it is going to the moon and has a lunar vehicle on board to research the moon's surface. The name of the space craft is called Chang'e after the princess and instead of having a lunar 'rover' (as the Americans and Russians) the Chinese have a lunar 'rabbit' because of the legend. It should land on the moon in mid-December ... I just hope they don't find any real Moon Cakes!!!

Lastly, I am going through the process of getting my Chinese work permit and resident's visa, and as usual each time I do this it is different, either because the national rules have changed, or the local province has decided to change things. The only constant is the medical, where, as I've told you several times before, it's a parade in and out of different specialist doctor offices, with varying degrees of thoroughness. Apparently they found all the right bits so I am now officially alive, also after much form filling I am now officially an 'expert' and have a passport-type book to prove it, valid for 3 years. As a General Manager I thought that I wasn't really an expert at anything (the clue is in the title!) but now obviously I'm an Expert General Manager. I know what some of you are thinking . . . he fits the other definition of an expert: EX , being a 'has been' and a SPURT is just a drip under pressure!!! Well, obtaining this Expert License is the next step to getting my Resident's visa, which I hope to have in the next 3 weeks.

I hope you are all getting prepared for Christmas since I expect the shops here to start gearing up in the next few days with assorted tinsel, tree shapes and cashiers being forced to wear various red stuff.

Best wishes to you all from Panda country,
Ma Ding

BACK FOR THE FESTIVE BIT –
17th December 2013

Well I'm in countdown mode now for getting home for Christmas and I hope I'll have time to catch up with some of you and maybe share a Yuletide dram.

Yesterday we had the first bit of real rain in the last 8 weeks although it had stopped by late morning. However when I ventured out to buy a heater for the apartment the pavements were really treacherous. You remember I explained about the wonderful pavement patterns with very slippery smooth marble interspersed with normal slabs. Well, now we have had eight weeks' worth of tyre rubber, car and motorbike oil on most pavements since they are used as additional carriageways and parking. Now going out for a walk is a bit like ice-skating as I lurch from tree to tree just in case I slip. In fact I did slip quite badly but managed with a lot of whirling arms to keep from falling onto my backside. The locals however must have thought that this strange foreigner was doing the latest western dance because I had some really odd looks and nobody rushed to help the poor old bloke. One of the differences is that the Chinese tend to walk quite slowly and often walk arm in arm . . . now I know why!!

Last week the bosses came to visit, both my old boss, Peter, who is retiring early, and the new one who is keen to stamp his authority on things. So we did a bit of a handover thing with me in the middle trying to be diplomatic by not blaming some of the major issues on the old boss but needing the new one to understand the problems I'm faced with. As it happens the new boss, Austen, has joined from David Brown Hydraulics, the sister company of the business I was with when I was working in Changzhou during 2010-2011. He knows many of the people that I knew from that time so we were able to have good chat about various old colleagues. A visit like this is very wearing in that I had to make sure that everything went like clockwork, not just the work stuff, but hotels, transport, meals, etc. It culminated in a banquet with my full team (only 23) as a farewell to one boss and welcoming another. As the host I gave my speech in Chinese with the translator doing the English, however it soon became apparent that my Chinese wasn't being well understood and the English translation wasn't much better, so we switched to me speaking English and the translator Chinese. It was quite fun though and I gave Peter a leaving gift of some famous Sichuan embroidery thing. The whole visit seemed to go well until Austen told me that the Chinese business was 'my train set' and I remarked that even so (to use the Thomas the Tank Engine analogy) he was the Fat Controller!! I think he saw the funny side.

I'm getting really fed up with our driver. We use a local company that has several cars and drivers, but the boss man has been our driver for over a year, picking Michael (my Production Manager) and me up every morning at 7.30am and taking us back in the evening. Well, every day except Thursday, because in a similar way to Hangzhou, Chengdu is trying to limit its rush hour traffic by restricting number plates on certain days. We have named our driver (real name Wang) Mr Slow, or 2K Tony. Why, because he drives this big black Chevrolet thing at never more than 2000 revs. This means that we have only gone about 5 yards when he changes from first to second gear, another 10 yards and we are up to third. You get the picture. I believe he thinks he's saving petrol but the engine just clunks and jerks along, even on the motorway in top gear he's only doing 75 kilometres an hour (about 47 mph), when the traffic allows. We've tried to tell him he's ruining the engine and could he please drive a little faster but to no avail. I'm told he used to drive trucks in the army so he's got into the habit. So although it's not a priority, we need to find a solution to this in the new year.

The single global culture moves steadily onwards as Christmas becomes ever more evident in China. I remember when I was young (yes I can still remember some things from that far back!) that Halloween wasn't a big thing, now it's a major event in the UK and China. Christmas is going the same way; another big selling opportunity! Yes the shops and restaurants are now all decked out with Christmas stuff with the staff all wearing red hats, etc. Every major shop has either a huge artificial Christmas tree outside or a giant blow-up Santa Claus. When I say artificial I don't mean looking a bit like a tree, I mean just some triangular structure with lots of lights and tinsel. In fact the 'tree' outside one shopping centre is made entirely of green plastic7-UP fizzy drink bottles, this

thing is at least 40ft high and they reckon made from 30,000 bottles!!! The shops are all playing the dreaded Christmas music on a never-ending loop, with each shop only having a maximum of two tunes, usually Jingle Bells and We Wish You a Merry Christmas. You know how it is that when your ears tune into a noise you can't block it out. It's the same with this stuff so I'm in and out of shops as quickly as possible now, buy the milk and veg and get away before I become a Jingled Bell! Bah Humbug!

Anyway, if I don't manage to catch up with you over the Christmas week let me take this opportunity to wish you and your families a very restful Christmas and a Happy 2014.

Best wishes and Jingle bells,
Ma Ding

BACK IN PANDA LAND! – 2nd January 2014

I did enjoy the few days I spent at home for Christmas and I managed to catch up with many of the Painswick bods. I trust you all had a relaxing Christmas and are looking forward to 2014, and after the torrential rain over Christmas I'm sure there will hosepipe bans in force by the summer.

I've arrived back to a foggy and cold Chengdu, the locals telling me that this weather has settled in and any movement will only get things colder. I think I'll have to buy another radiator for the apartment, but I did bring my thermals back, along with socks, hankies and loads of chocolate for the winter evenings watching odd DVDs.

I forgot to mention in my previous note that we had the David Cameron visit to Chengdu just before Christmas. He, along with 150 'British Business Leaders' and some other Government staff, descended on our fair city to supposedly find out what it was like doing business in the west of China and what opportunities there were. I was invited along to a few meetings where a few of us locals were asked questions by the great and the good. It was all a bit rushed and seemed more for show without any real substance. Whilst we were hosted by the Deputy Mayor of Chengdu and were talking to the other members of his entourage, the man Cameron was being wined and dined by the Mayor in another part of the city. It has to be said that Cameron did get some very good publicity on the Chinese TV during and after his visit and he left a good impression of the UK. However, my feeling from the other members of the tour was that it was an interesting 'jolly' and that the most value came from talking to their fellow travelers on the chartered jumbo jet. They might just as well have been locked together in a Birmingham hotel for 3 days!! As usual the Chinese don't miss a trick when there is money to be made: the restaurant in Chengdu where the Prime Minister enjoyed the famous Sichuan Hot Pot meal has made the 'Cameron Menu' available at 800 Yuan (about £80) and if you want to be looked after by his actual waitress that will be another £20!!! I'm told it's quite popular (at the moment).

Fog! I've not seen anything this bad for years. We would probably call it a 'pea-souper', the Chinese call it 'fikphog'. Anyway today the expressway was closed so we had to drive the back roads into the factory. A nightmare!! Well, Mr Slow (my driver) is cautious at the best of times but in this weather he just crawled along swapping lanes willy-nilly and getting lots of tootings from other frustrated drivers. So, some observations of Chinese fog driving ... Firstly you know those fog light things on most, if not all cars; they are not used in China, instead most drivers put their hazard warning lights on so all you can see is lots of amber flashing lights. The downside of this is that no-one knows if or when another driver is indicating to turn a corner or change lane. And another thing, you know that most city roads have at least 6 lanes plus cycle/scooter lanes, well this makes the roads very wide. I had not noticed before but at the crossroads the traffic lights are only on the far side of the road, not above you as well, as they are in the UK. And yes, in the fog you just cannot see the red traffic light on the other side (the green is just about visible) so the crossroads are just a mess until the police come along and make things worse!! So what do the local drivers do? The roads are all clogged up so there is only one place to drive, and that is along the pavements until they hit cyclists coming the other way since there is no direction discipline on pavements in China. Took me an hour and a half to get into work this morning. I hope it's cleared a bit by the time I go home.

Talking of work, as you know we are opening a new factory to support a major customer in China with large metal parts for their MRI scanners. These products have to be made to very tight tolerances so we have new machines being installed and lots of support from our UK parent company where they have several years' experience manufacturing the same parts. However, you know that most things in life shrink when it gets cold (I can think of a couple that don't!), well it's the same with metal and in the very cold weather we are currently having it causes us lots of problems. The factory area is not heated at all and has been at about zero centigrade for the last few days. So we machine these things to the dimensions on the drawing then move them to the quality inspection room (which is heated) only to find that they are growing bigger as they warm up. So now they are too big, we take them back and take more metal off. So it's all a bit trial and error at the moment. (I know the techies amongst you will be saying that we should be calculating temperature offsets, I'll just say that the size, shape and method of fabrication means that normal rules don't apply!!). This is not a problem in the UK because their factory area is heated and we will have the opposite problem in the summer months when it can get up to 40 degrees centigrade and we don't have air conditioning in the workshop. Just another issue that wasn't considered at the outset.

So it's now 2014. It really doesn't seem that long ago that we were celebrating the new millenium, where has the time gone? Are we older and wiser, or just older?

Wishing you all a wonderful 2014,
Your man with the pandas
Ma Ding

CHINESE NEW YEAR AND ALL THAT JAZZ
– 24th January 2014

Well here we go again, the Chinese New Year palarva!! There is now a 14 day 'holiday' period where everyone is travelling back to their home towns. This all kicked off last week, although the actual main celebration day is the 30th January the Chinese world won't really settle down again until sometime during the week of the 10th February. Travel costs have gone through the roof, if you can get tickets! So a normal £50 flight ticket is about £200 and the high speed train tickets are like gold dust. In fact there are only 3 days official holiday, but we will be working the Sunday before and the Saturday after to add another couple of days. Then if you live outside the province where you work there's an extra couple of days travel allowance, and then of course people have been saving up some of their personal days, and even taken unpaid leave to really extend the break. The bottom line is that most businesses will be on short working for the best part of two weeks. I had my Christmas break so I'll only be off for 5 days (3 plus Sat and Sun) and although I initially thought of going to somewhere different the cost quickly set me straight. So I will have a few days relaxing and exploring more of the Chengdu sights.

The New Year will be the year of the horse, yes, my Chinese name (ma = horse) so it should be a very good year for me I am told!!! There are pictures, models and animations of horses all over the place, which together with the normal Chinese red lanterns and other guff makes everywhere look worse than the naff Christmas decorations. Someone even pasted a big red poster to the front door of my apartment. I've no idea what it says, maybe 'happiness and health' or 'go home you big nose foreigner'!!

On Wednesday we had our company party for all 23 employees. So that meant a couple of tables at a local hot pot restaurant with lots of beer being consumed with the normal 'ganbei' (bottoms up) toasts all around. The highlight was the lucky dip where prizes from £100 were awarded, not bad odds with 8 prizes and only 20 people. As the boss it was my duty to pick out the winners so obviously I have now split the staff into supporters (the winners) and enemies (the losers). Then it was all on to the Karaoke bar for a couple of hours of horrendous warbling. Luckily there weren't too many English songs so we Brits got off lightly. Having said that I did manage a strange rendition of a famous Chinese song called yueliangdaobiao, reading most of the words off the screen in Chinese and hitting at least one note in three. I did get an applause from the mainly drunken troops. One of the Chinese female workers, our senior welder, clearly has a voice that goes with her looks, a fog horn comes to mind! But at least she got into the spirit of things whereas some of the other staff went very quiet after the beer and wine.

I have noticed that compared to other cities in China, Chengdu seems to have a higher number of police on the streets and metro system. I'm told it's mainly as a result of being close to Tibet and having a large Tibetan population in the city. You may have noticed over the years that policemen are getting bigger and bigger belts to carry all their stuff. It used to be only the truncheon and handcuffs, then extended to Walkie-Talkie, gun and Taser. Well the Chinese policeman's pride of place, positioned for a quick draw on his shiny black leather belt, is none other than his flask of green tea. The efficiency of whipping it out, taking a slurp and replacing it is a wonder to behold. Whereas I suspect he would struggle to get the gun or truncheon out in double that time. Perhaps if push comes to shove, he would be better bashing the criminal over the head with the tea flask!!

My new boss and his boss, the Group CEO from the UK, turned up last week and, as ever, had to be looked after in the evenings as well. So, a very full week but not feeling as though much was achieved. However they were very impressed to see how good the new factory looked since their last visit towards the end of last year. So we all got pats on the back 'You've all done very well' type comments and a long list of actions to get on with before next time. In all honesty, the speed with which we have turned a bare shell into a proper business facility is amazing, something only possible in China. We now have to think about an official opening with lion dances, lots of fireworks, local dignitaries etc. With Chinese New Year fast approaching and knowing that I'll have a few sleepless nights with all the fireworks being let off around the city, the last thing I want to consider is even more of the same stuff!!! Or am I just an old killjoy?

I hope you have all survived the floods that according to the Chinese news broadcasts have isolated most of the UK countryside.

Best wishes and a Happy Chinese New Year, or as we say Gong Xi Fa Cai (wealth and happiness),
Ma Ding

BACK TO NORMAL??? – February 7th 2014

The Chinese New Year event is now thankfully over and the world is getting back to normal, or as normal as life is here in Chengdu! It was really odd being around, but not having much to do over the holiday. On New Year's Eve, it was quiet in the morning with most of the smaller shops closing up and only some large shops open so that people could buy the last-minute stuff. By mid-afternoon it was oddly quiet with hardly a car on the road, and then about 8ish all hell broke loose. Fireworks everywhere. It seemed that one of the main launch pads was the area outside the Carrefour supermarket opposite my apartment. The noise went on until about 4 in the morning, so I was not a happy bunny the next day, not helped by losing a large filling whilst chewing on some of China's world famous sticky beef!!! The fireworks continued for several days and due to the fact that most of the municipal workers were on holiday, no-one was clearing up the firework mess, so there were red bits and burnt cardboard everywhere you walked.

Not many of you will know that at one time I thought about being a toothwright (dentist). So much so that I even started doing the appropriate A-levels until my lack of affinity for Chemistry made me rethink, so I changed courses and got on the engineering track, and the rest as they say is history! Well, I've described to you before the problem of Chinese dentistry, most of it happens outside, or in small open-plan shops for all the passers-by to see. Added to the fact is that the Hepatitis B problem in China (about 15% of the population) is often put down to poor dental health. So although I don't have a major problem going to a Chinese doctor, there was no way that I was going to a Chinese dentist. So I thought, I'm an engineer, dentistry is mechanical, so I'll do some DIY!! This was a biggish filling in a troublesome tooth, lower right side (do you really want to know this?). The obvious, simple solution is to glue the old filling back in with superglue. So I bought the glue, but then had visions of me holding the filling between my fingers, squeezing some the glue onto the filling, then positioning it in the cavity (technical word!), only to find my finger also glued to my teeth. Not wishing to look a complete prat and go to a hospital with a finger stuck in my mouth I had to plan another solution. First glue half a cocktail stick to the upper side of the filling, then position it without glue and use a pen to put a mark on the cocktail stick to confirm the correct orientation. Add mirror, strong light and plenty of tissues to ensure the mouth is kept dry. Next put glue on the underside of the filling and go for it! Finally when the glue is set, break off the cocktail stick. In hindsight the whole thing was fraught with possible problems but in the event it all worked OK and the filling has remained in place for over a week. The ol' 'I can fix anything' Martyn mentality, or is it the 'too mean to pay someone else'? So with the lack of NHS dentists and private ones costing a fortune, is a new career path opening up? (or not!).

I took myself off to Chongqing for a couple of days during the Chinese New Year holiday. It's a 2-hour fast train ride from Chengdu and the point where the Yangtse and Jiang rivers meet. It is also one of the largest metropolitan conurbations in the world with about 30 million people and famous for being the main beneficiary of the Three Gorges Dam project. I wanted to see where the rivers meet because they are supposed to be two completely different colours; also to visit the Three Gorges Museum (at some stage I want to do the Three Gorges river cruise) and a couple of other recommended sights. On arrival at Chongqing railway station and then taking the metro to the city centre I got the feeling that this city is still being constructed, with many new skyscrapers going up everywhere. Are they really intent on creating a centre where the population is greater than most countries? However it has to be said that the city centre itself was very impressive with smart buildings and pedestrian areas with lots of trees. Chongqing is also quite hilly which made a pleasant change from the total flatness of Chengdu. Walking down to where these two large rivers joined was a disappointment, whether it was because the weather was overcast so everything seemed grey, or possibly from my low

212

viewpoint (not just because I'm short!!), but I could not see any difference in the colour of the rivers, they just merged together in an area probably more than twice the width of the Thames in London.

The Three Gorges Museum was very interesting, showing the ancient history of the area before it was completely changed in 2003 by flooding the whole area and displacing over one million people. The propaganda photos of farmers and village people 'willingly moving from their family homes for the greater good of the Chinese nation' was evident everywhere. China has a water availability problem many times greater than some western countries and rightly or wrongly they have the capability to sort it out. In this case, enabling many millions of people in central China to have access to water all year round. One of the other exhibition rooms in this museum was dedicated to the anti-Japanese history in the area. Chongqing was a centre for the Japanese occupation of China and some ferocious fighting between Japan and the Allies (mainly American and Chinese troops) during the Second World War. If you've been watching the recent news you will know that these feelings are still very evident today.

Walking close to a park near my apartment last weekend I kept hearing loud cracking noises followed by a strange humming sound. I went to investigate and saw two old codgers playing with large spinning tops which they kept going with large whips. When the tops reached a particular speed they emitted this deep humming sound. The whips were made from a piece of leather about 3 feet long attached to a wooden rod of a similar length. These old guys seemed to adopt a pose similar to a golf swing before spinning round to strike the top. Could this be a new golf training aid or just practice for keeping the wife in order!

I hope you are all keeping your heads above water (in the flooded areas).

Best wishes,
Martyn

GONE TO THE DOGS – 21st February 2014

This city of Chengdu seems to be the dog city of China, dogs are everywhere. When I first came to China and was based in the southern city of Liuzhou, dog was the standard winter meat and the only dogs to be seen were those in cages ready for cooking. Very occasionally someone would have a small pet poodle on a lead and the obvious joke was about takeaway ready meals! However dogs in Chengdu seem to be something of a status symbol. In the same way that lots of rich Chinese have Bentleys, Rollers and Ferraris to declare their wealth to the world, (even though there is no way of driving the car properly on the congested roads), so dog owners delight in showing off their pooches by roaming the streets and parks. They often sit in very crowded areas with their big, beautifully groomed dog held close as if to say, "Look at me, I can afford *not* to eat this big dog"! Very close to my apartment there are 3 'poodle parlours' where you can see a constant stream of dog owners waiting to get their pets

What a bright doggy.

groomed, with even the hair being coloured various odd shades of blue and yellow. Also, because it is cold at the moment many dogs have brightly coloured jackets and even bootees for some of them. It's probably a great life being a dog in Chengdu, not only do you get pampered but you

214

seem to be free to do your 'business' wherever you want and there's loads of interesting smells to sniff out and investigate (and that's just the people)!! As you know the Chinese for hello is 'nihao' so when I meet a dog I often say "Ni hound"!! (Sorry).

So it's not just the shihtsu (originally a Chinese breed of dog, why am I not surprised by the name?) on the streets that's causing the pollution at the moment. With very little rain or wind in Chengdu the muck just gets moved around a little bit. There has been such bad pollution in Beijing over the last few weeks it has become a major issue. For the technical amongst you the main measurement standard is for particles of 2.5 microns or less, with an internationally recognised AQI (Air Quality Index) safe level of below 50. The level in the Cotswolds last time I looked was about 7, so very good (you lucky people!). The level in many medium-sized cities with lots of cars generally gets to about 50-100 which is termed 'moderate' pollution. However, Beijing has been up around 450 which is termed 'hazardous', i.e. it will affect everybody's health, not just those with breathing problems. There's a good website that's worth looking at if you want to see the pollution levels around the world www.aqicn.org. Chengdu at this time of year is regularly up at 200 or so, 'unhealthy', so we are waiting for the rainy season to give us some clearer air. You've got lots of rain in the UK, why hog it all, don't be so selfish and send some over to us! Thanks in advance.

When I first came to Chengdu back in 2007, to meet a supplier, they took me to visit two world heritage sites; a 2000-year-old irrigation complex and also the famous mountain devoted to Taoism (or Daoism if you prefer). At that time we just rolled up to the entrance of both these tourist attractions, parked the car for free, paid probably about 2 pounds to get in and could wander around as we wished without too many other visitors getting in the way. It really was quite interesting and I climbed to the top of this mountain (Qingshenshan) without meeting too many others. So the other weekend I took one of the UK visitors on the same trip, only using a Chengdu tour company coach from the city centre. Well, in 7 years things have changed! The growing tourist industry in China with significant increases in both Chinese and foreign visitors has meant that both these attractions were to my mind a lot less attractive. Firstly you couldn't get close to the entrance in a car, bicycle or a coach. We parked about a mile away and had to queue up for little electric buses to take us to the entrances I remembered from 7 years ago. Then obviously it cost a lot more to get in. But probably the worst aspect at both places was that so many areas had been turned over to selling souvenirs and foody things. Even the temples up the mountain had kiosks selling crap (food and souvenirs!!). The previous time it would only be the occasional toothless old man or woman trying to sell us a local cucumber type thing half-way up the mountain. Also, I remembered being impressed with the rough and ready stone steps going up the mountain, worn down by several hundred years of monks and disciples climbing up to pray in the temples. Now most of the steps have been replaced by standard concrete so that the Chinese ladies who wear stilettos and carry their Gucci handbags won't fall over!! Seriously you won't believe what some of the locals were wearing to spend a couple of hours climbing a mountain. Anyway, I'm glad I have been able to visit many places in China before they lost their charm and got turned into major commercial opportunities.

Work's pretty tough at the moment with lots of pressure from the parent company to get the older of the 2 businesses I run profitable, and also get the new one up and running so we can start selling product. At the same time the Chinese customers are demanding price reductions! Normal ol' stuff really with lots of interesting negotiations. I think China is starting to realise that it isn't as competitive in the world as it used to be and is seriously looking to manage cost and wages. So the happy days of pay increases of more than 10% per year are rapidly coming to an end. We are about to do the pay review with our folks, so I expect many to be disappointed.

Not much else to report other than all the excitement on

216

Chinese TV caused by the Winter Olympics. Obviously they focus on all the events where the Chinese are doing well, and don't mention any less-than-favourable results. For instance, when China narrowly beat Team GB in the men's curling the whole match was live and the final winning stone by the Chinese team was shown time and time again for 2 days. However yesterday when their team lost to the Canadians in the semi-finals there has been hardly a mention. I guess we are just as partisan with our coverage, if indeed it is being shown on UK television. Now if there was a wading through floods event . . .

Best wishes to you all,
Ma, avoiding the dog poo, Ding

RAGS TO RICHES – 19th March 2014

I've had a couple of complaints from some of the elder recipients of my emails stating that the text is too small for their failing eyesight. So I've increased the font size a bit … I hope this helps. Now with modern technology I could of course leave you with audio or video messages. Maybe in the future you could get the real message experience with 3D video, surround sound and smellovision (probably not good from China!). On second thoughts I think it's best just to continue as before, then at least you have the option of pressing the delete key.

Back on the old theme of cars and local driving skills. So, as I've mentioned before there are loads of very expensive cars in Chengdu, particularly Bentleys and Maseratis, although Ferraris, Lamborghinis and Rollers are also regularly seen creeping along at 5 mph. I noticed over Chinese New Year, lots of cars, expensive and otherwise, with what can only be described as red rags tied around the wing mirrors. I thought this was some sort of cultural sign for good luck, or wealth and happiness. However your intrepid investigator has now discovered the reality. These red rags, which are about 6 inches long (15cm in new money), flap around when the cars get up to speed and act as a wiper/cleaner for the wing mirrors. They obviously wear out after a while and look pretty grubby. So now I understand why a rich Chinese person, who has a fairly new, bright and shiny Bentley (in puke green colour) has grubby red rags hanging from each wing mirror. Something about function over style, or just too lazy to replace with new rags? Obviously they don't need to be a red colour to work, so feel free to try it out in your area with your favourite colour, maybe it will catch on!

Motorway (expressway) driving around this city seems to be much more aggressive than my experience in other areas of China, and this coupled to no lane discipline, poorly maintained vehicles and overloaded trucks is a recipe for problems. Last Monday on the way home we had just got onto the expressway when it all came to a stop, and then we crawled along for the next hour. Mr Slow, our driver, just

At speed the red rag cleans the mirror

bobbles along letting everyone cut in front of him so you can guess how frustrated I was getting, as it felt like we were going backwards. Through all this pushing in we went past three minor accidents before we finally came to the main cause of the problem; two smallish trucks overloaded with wooden planks. One truck was turned over on its back and facing the wrong way, the other was caught up in the central reservation, with police and drivers gesticulating wildly. Then a little way further on there was another crash where someone had clearly been trying to make up for lost time and hit a slower vehicle whilst overtaking. So because of the aggressive driving style one serious accident turned into a total of five problems causing extra delays and even more aggressive driving. It will only get worse, as in Chengdu there are about 4,000 new cars coming onto the roads every week.

Oh, and still on the car subject, we were held up again a couple of weeks ago on the expressway as a wedding procession of about 8 cars all decked out in ribbons and stuff decided to drive in convoy in the middle lane at 20mph with their horns blaring. Do you think I wished the happy couple a wonderful future together? Would you if you were going to be late for your spicy fish head with rice?

Friday night brought gale force winds howling around the apartment which meant it was very difficult to sleep, but Saturday morning turned out to be a fine spring day with clear blue skies. The wind had done its job and pushed the pollution somewhere else. In fact the weekend was the best weather since I've been in this city and very pleasant. Walking round the city (I was trying to buy a new pair of shoes) I noticed that in most of the smaller streets the mahjong tables had been brought out onto the pavements with crowds gathering round the players to view the tactics. In a couple of places it seemed to get quite rowdy as I think various bets were being placed, and I always thought it seemed such a nice game!!! Also out in force during this fine weather are the old men with their birds (no not Chinese girls!), small parrots and singing birds that are kept in small round cages and hung from trees in the small park areas close to the main roads. Personally I think it's just another excuse to get out of the house, away from the wife and be able to have a fag and a relaxing chat with a few mates, a bit like fishing or golf!!! Whether they can hear each other with all the chirping going on I'm not sure, but they did seem a happy bunch of old men whiling away the hours.

As you know the Chinese writing are pictograms with each character usually meaning a word. We westerners of course have individual letters which are arranged to make a word. Now when a Chinese marketing company makes an advertising sign using Chinese characters they are usually very neatly arranged with some gaps to make the meanings a little clearer. However if the same company is used to do the sign in English I have noticed that the concept of letters forming words is not understood and so the letters are arranged as if they were characters with individual meanings. (Is this a bit complicated?). Well, what I'm getting to is that occasionally you see an English sign where the words have been split up and the sense is lost. In this respect I saw this sign on a hoarding last week, in Chinese and then below on 2 lines, the first line being DINGS GROWTH ASS and the second line ET COMPANY LTD. Unfortunately, it had disappeared a couple of days later, I expect someone had pointed out the obvious error . . . that an apostrophe was required before the S in Dings!!!

I'm trying to get things sorted so that I can get back to the UK before the end of May. But because we are only 20 people running 2 businesses where there are lots of start-up and customer demands finding a suitable time is difficult. Hopefully I will get something booked in the next 2-3 weeks, or I will miss the Cotswold spring. (Is that similar to the Arab spring? are you all revolting?)

Best wishes to you all,
mahjong Mart

BACK FROM OZ – 22nd April 2014

I know that I said in the last missive that I was hoping to get back sometime in May, well that has all changed because I decided to give Julie a surprise and gatecrash her holiday to Australia to see Amy. I was only in Melbourne for a week and in spite of the poor weather (drizzle every day) it was good to catch up with Julie and Amy and also to get some clean air into my lungs!! Returning to Chengdu the temperature has picked up and it's now a very pleasant 20-25 Centigrade although it does get a bit rainy at this time of the year. In a couple of months' time it will become really hot and muggy, so I hope the air-con system works in my apartment.

So spring is sprung and the trees have started to sprout shiny new bright green leaves, however in a couple of weeks they will turn dark and dirty due to the pollution ... moan, moan, moan!!

Children ... who'd have 'em? Well the Chinese obviously, and they are now starting to relax the one child policy so that in a few years' time there are more workers to support the aging population in their pensionable years. What I have noticed during my wanderings around this city are quite a lot of twins aged about 2-5 years old. In fact there are two sets in my apartment complex and I often see others most weekends. So what is going on? Well when I was working in Liuzhou one of the project managers, a woman called Annie, told me that although she already had a little girl, her father, who was a doctor, was going to make sure she had a boy in the near future. When I asked how he could make this happen I was given some rubbish about special Chinese medicine. Best not to enquire too deeply, but clearly certain couples in Chengdu are finding a way to obtain twins so they can have two children without paying a heavy fine. Even the Chinese government wouldn't impose a fine on an 'accident of birth'. However, to me it doesn't feel like it's always an accident! The Chinese have a world-wide reputation for copying things (DVDs, watches, handbags etc.) so why not children? Is one of the twins real and the other a clone or are they both clones? Tough questions for modern times!!!

Talking of children, I had my first Chinese car crash a few days ago. In the early evening I was strolling through a pedestrian area not far from my apartment when I got hit by a young boy driving his little electric toy car. He must have only been 4 or 5 years old but was already terrorising the pedestrians in his bright yellow vehicle. In my day we had to work hard with pedals to go anywhere, now these small cars are fully powered and seem to go quite quickly, a bit like a small bumper car. I suppose I was more shocked than hurt as he ran into the back of my legs, his mother (or granny?) shouted at him, or it could have been me she was angry with for being in the way of little Zhongy's driving experience. As the weather gets better there will be more of these things driven by out-of-control children in the pedestrian areas and so, along with normal cars occupying the pavements, I will be back in the gutters yet again! In any case it seems to me that they are starting to get the bad driving habits at a very early age so there's probably no hope for the future of the Chinese traffic!!

You heard it here first … the new trend in shoes as seen twice in Hong Kong during my journey back from Oz. Teenage girls wearing different colour shoes on each foot, with pastel colours seeming to be preferred. As most of you know I have worn odd socks for many years and it largely goes un-noticed because people don't often look down. However shoes are a bit more obvious. I haven't yet worked out whether these odd colour shoes were bought as a pair, or if the girls in question (who were not together) bought 2 pairs to mix and match, or had a mate with the same shoe in a different colour so one could be borrowed. I will have to investigate more thoroughly, or maybe it's not that important in the context of the current world problems!!!

Last Friday I had to go to the big Medical Equipment exhibition in Shenzhen (the mainland city opposite Hong Kong), firstly to meet with one customer, but also to try to find new potential customers. The whole area around the exhibition centre was swarming with people, and as I hadn't been able to pre-register as a visitor the queues to get in were horrendous. However, when there is money to be made there will be a Chinaman somewhere, so I wasn't surprised to be approached by people selling exhibitor's passes which hang around your neck with a barcode to allow you to be scanned for entry. So I paid one pound for this exhibitor's pass which, apart from saying Sales Director in big letters, was covered in lots of Chinese writing. So for all I know I could have been the Sales Director of a haemorrhoid extraction equipment company!! Luckily I wasn't questioned by the guard who scanned my pass and so I easily bypassed a lengthy queue.

Whilst in Shenzhen I noticed lots of people wearing American stars and stripes clothing and carrying bags with similar designs. This is in contrast to Chengdu where there seems to be a preference for our Union Jack (flag) designs on mini cars, scooters, T-shirts and bags. Maybe it's because David Cameron visited the city last December and now the local Chinese think that they look cool in the British flag colours. I know that if Angela Merkel visited Cheltenham I certainly wouldn't rush out and buy a shirt in Germany's colours. Anyway, back to Shenzhen with the American theme, I did see a few shops selling this American stuff; T-shirts with Harvard University or Washington D.C. written on it. Then I actually passed a burly Chinese guy wearing a shirt with the words Camp David written in white. He looked very pleased with himself, but I expect he didn't get the alternative meaning, I'm sure he wouldn't have bought a shirt with Butch Eric written on it!!

I'm hearing that the weather has improved in the UK so I trust you all had a great Easter break and are now enjoying the spring sunshine after a pretty dismal winter. Do you know, not one choccy Easter egg to be found anywhere in Chengdu, and I did look hard!

Best wishes and g'day to you all,
Ma Ding

LIFT CULTURE – 14th May 2014

A few days ago it was the British Chamber of Commerce (South West China) AGM and as a member of this exalted organisation I was invited to attend and vote for the new committee members. The event was held in a swanky hotel in the southern suburbs of Chengdu and was attended by several hundred of the great and the good, including some officials from the British Chamber China HQ in Beijing. I duly arrived and was ushered into the queue to sign in where I was given a large purple flower for my buttonhole that apparently indicated that I was indeed a fully paid-up member and therefore entitled to vote. Many of the others were not adorned with this ghastly flower and so I concluded that they were only there for the beer etc. I was then taken to stand next to some poor bloke who was dressed up as a Buckingham Palace guardsman sporting a replica busby and standing in front of a London-based scene covering the wall. I then had my official photo taken. As I whispered to this young man that I felt a bit of a prat having my photo taken in this way, he said, "How do you think I feel? I've had to

You'd think you were really in London

stand here for over an hour and the hat's so small it keeps falling off if I move." I wandered off and watched a steady stream of Chinese delighted to have their picture taken with the replica guardsman!!

All canapés and fizzy for the next hour as I chatted to various people, some of whom were lobbying for my vote. Then it was into the ballroom for the main event: food, cabaret and the voting! I ended up sitting quite a distance from the stage on a very mixed table, Europeans and Chinese. The very well-spoken lady sitting on my right was a teacher at one of the international schools who, together with her husband (who was very wisely at home looking after the dogs!), had arrived in China last year from a couple of years working in Kazakhstan. The young Chinese waiter arrived with the wine and proceeded to pour a minute amount into each glass. This is typical, as I think I've mentioned before, in Chinese restaurants they only cover the bottom of the glass with the red wine, and it's not for the taste test, it's every time. You just don't get enough for a nice slurp! So fairly quickly I explained to matey that he should pour a reasonable amount into each glass, and, honestly, we wouldn't drink it any quicker!! As if!! Then came various speeches to firstly show how well the Chamber had or hadn't done last year, and secondly to give a chance to the prospective candidates to promote themselves. It has to be said that the acoustics in the room were rubbish so that after about 15 minutes the back half of the room was not even trying listen and just talking and drinking. This then made it more difficult for most of the other tables to hear so that only a very select few at the front of the room were eventually following proceedings. Finally the western-type meal, which was actually quite good, commenced, but each course was interspersed by a round of voting, with the winner of the previous vote being announced prior to the next round of voting. So it started to become a bit complicated as the people who lost the vote to be president then became eligible to be vice-president, and the people who lost out at vice-president level became eligible as secretary, and so on down through various offices until it appeared that all of those standing for office had a job, even if it was bog-standard committee member. Is this democracy?? As usual at these events, having been persuaded to buy some raffle tickets, it was now time for the prize draw. The lady to my right had actually purchased quite a lot. In the course of earlier conversation she was explaining to me that she and "her husband" only ever fly business class because "it's just so demeaning travelling economy". And you've guessed it, she only won the first prize; a pair of British Airways return tickets from Chengdu to London, economy class. I did of course explain that since they were not business class tickets, she obviously couldn't use them, so perhaps she could give them to me. She gave me a bit of a cold stare, so I made my leave, congratulating the new President on his election success on the way out.

I've discovered a golf range about a 20-minute walk from my apartment. It's in a complex which has several tennis, badminton and table-tennis facilities, including the emergency meeting point in the event of another earthquake (2008 and early 2013). So I turned up and walked to the entrance of this 3-storey building. I know that in China golf is a rich man's sport and the car park in front of the building did nothing to dispel this as there were two bright white Lamborghinis, a couple of Bentleys and several Porsches, Maseratis and Mercs. Explaining that I wanted to hit a few balls and didn't have my own clubs, I was given a 7 iron and a very large basket of balls in exchange for Rmb130 (about 13 quid). I then wandered into the range itself which had about 40 bays on the ground floor, each with a table and chair, mirror to check your swing action (or make-up!) and a cold face flannel in case you get over exerted!! So in total there were probably over 100 bays on the 3 floors. This was mid-Sunday morning and the place was packed, but I did manage to find a spare bay down at one end next to a middle-aged chap who clearly had all the gear; bright yellow shirt and beige 'Rupert Bear' golf trousers, together with a huge set of golf clubs. Unfortunately he didn't have too much of a clue as to how to hit the ball. On the other side was a young lad in a T-shirt and jeans belting the balls a long, long way. In front of us were the usual distance flags and then about 300 yards away was another 3-storey building with golfers hitting balls back at us. Luckily there was no-one of the Tiger Woods capability, because I'm sure they or we were in range!!! So I hit a few balls (not very well to start with) and then sat down for rest and to wipe my brow with the cold flannel. Watching, I noticed most of the golfers had a bit of a routine; hit about 20 balls, sit down and have a cigarette, hit a few more balls then summon the young gel to bring some tea, together with another ciggy. Followed by a wander up the range looking at others, then return for another few hits, tea and a cigarette. Have a chat on the mobile phone whilst smoking and drinking tea, etc. etc. I got the feeling that most of them were there for a good couple of hours whereas I was out in about 45 minutes, having taken my time. I'll definitely try to find a less busy time when I next feel the urge to hit some golf balls.

Hotel and apartment lifts in China seem to have their own unique culture. In the West on entering a lift the norm is to stand near the back wall facing the door and wait silently to arrive at the correct level, exit then carry on as normal. The only group of Chinese that seem to follow this rule are the very old, who shuffle in, turn round in readiness for exit and watch in silence as the floor numbers go by, waiting to shuffle out again. They are also the most polite, and usually acknowledge my presence with a nod of the head. The rest of the Chinese use the lifts as if everything was just continuing, barging in talking loudly, eating, drinking and smoking (even though most lifts have large signs forbidding smoking). If they are waiting to get in, they will ignore the normal convention of allowing those to exit first. So it's all a bit of a fight really! Worst moments for me are waiting for a hotel lift where you know there has been a wedding party; the lift arrives, the doors open and first thing out is the smell of baijiu (pronounced BY GEE OH), the local fire water which smells like bitter petrol fumes. Obviously I wait, in the hope that people contributing to the smell will also exit, but often they don't so I then have to squeeze in and get funny looks and probably welcoming words which are very slurred. The other nasty is getting into a fullish lift, standing close to, and facing the doors and then hearing from behind my shoulder a loud hawking sound as someone is preparing to have a good spit. Will they, or won't they? Can it be contained until they exit? Help!!! Also a lot of the folks in my apartment block have electric motor bikes which they keep in their apartments, even though there seems to be plenty of underground parking spaces. Since they use the lifts to transport these motor bikes, again I have to manoeuvre carefully so as not to get covered in mud and oil from the bikes. All great fun!!!

Other than that, it seems to be warming up now during the daytime and we are getting regular thunderstorms at night which, although interrupting my beauty (??) sleep, often cleans the air a bit for the next day.

I hope all is well in Blighty and summer is on its way at last.

Best wishes,
Ma Ding

ENGLAND 4 – ITALY 0, (ha ha!) – 10th JUNE 2014

And I thought that being thousands of miles away would spare me the FIFA World Cup razzamataz. No, you've guessed it, World Cup fever has now hit China and even though it is a minority sport, the opportunity to make some commercial gain never goes unmissed. So both outside and inside the local supermarkets gangs of assistants are on hand to give you a prize if you happen to score a goal in the elaborately arranged net. Outside my nearest supermarket (Carrefour) there is the famous Harbin beer brand trying to attract youths (with rich parents) to kick a golden ball somewhere towards a net and in the process win a golden can of beer and hopefully buy a crate-load or two!! Inside the shop there are several smaller displays requiring you to get a ball in the back of the net and thereby win some choccy or biscuits. It appears that there is nothing healthy to be gained by playing these games, however they do seem reasonably busy. It has to be said that escaped balls are all over the place, providing a tripping hazard for the unwary. I have to admit I did buy a couple of packs of beer so I would have something cool to drink when I come home from a hard, hot day at work!!! Whether anyone here will actually have the chance to watch any of the live football from Brazil, I'm not sure. Firstly unless China is actually involved it very rarely

Kick a goal and win a beer.

shows the event, and secondly the time difference (11 hours) means that the matches are on at very unsociable hours. No doubt England will surprise us all with a wonderful display of average skills and injuries before losing to the Germans on penalties. I'm not holding my breath!!

Our normal driver Mr Slow had a few days off a couple of weeks ago, so a different driver picked me up from the new factory day and proceeded to take me back to the city centre. He was a very jolly fellow with a big smile only matched by the big gap in his teeth. As he was driving along I noticed he was watching the centre console a lot, and where on modern cars you normally have the radio or sat nav, in this car there was a television screen which was showing live news. Now in the UK and Europe I believe that if a TV is fitted to a car it should automatically turn off when the car is moving. Well I think in China, either there is no such rule or matey had found a way of disconnecting the auto-off since we were travelling along at 60+ kph and he was still reasonably glued to the screen, or turning round to give me a toothless grin. After two or three miles of this I decided it was pretty unsafe so I told him to turn it off or he wasn't getting paid, which he did reluctantly. The car was a black Chinese make called a BYD. In all the adverts BYD seems to stand for 'Build Your Dreams' however after this experience I reckon its 'Blimey You're Dangerous'!! (I've obviously kept it clean, but you can try to make up some others).

I'm not sure if I've mentioned it before but usually one evening a week I help a Chinese guy improve his English before he moves with his family to London in July. His name is Edward Liang and he is going to London to do a PhD in Manchurian studies. It seems that some of the best ancient Manchurian documents are to be found in the British Museum and some other UK collections, so it's easier for him to do this course in London. I have tried to explain that London is a fairly expensive place to live but it seems he has some sponsorship from a Beijing university and they will also help with his accommodation. We usually meet in a Westernish restaurant called Red River, which has a mixture of food from around the world, including typical Chinese dishes, Thai curries, hamburgers, pizzas and sandwiches. Last week I thought I'd be simple (aren't I always!!) and ordered macaroni cheese since the picture of the dish looked quite appetising. (Most menus in Chinese restaurants have lots of pictures of the food, not that they always resemble the actual thing served up!). A few minutes later the waitress proudly plonked down in front of me a plate of some greyish coloured penne pasta topped with a bit of grated cheese. I immediately tried to explain that this was not macaroni cheese, but soon came up against the Chinese logic of 'it's pasta and cheese and what's the problem if the pasta is a different shape?' The boss arrived, so again I tried to explain that in Italy (well not only Italy) if you order a particular type of pasta, that is what you expect, not something that's a totally different shape and texture. I think I only finally won the argument when we all looked closely at the photograph in the menu and decided both the pasta and the sauce were not the same. They explained that they didn't have any other different pasta so would I like to order something else? Since by this time the penne cheese thing had gone cold and congealed on the plate (the plate could be held vertically and nothing would budge), I decided to order a mushroom risotto on the basis that the Chinese do cook rice regularly. Actually by the time the risotto thing arrived I'd lost the will to live and Edward, my Chinese companion, had finished his burger a long time ago. I think we will try somewhere else next week.

I'm due back home next week so I'm hoping that the weather bucks up a bit. Actually on reflection I don't care since I'll be happy enough to breathe some clean air and see the horizon. Because I went to Australia in April there's a whole host of stuff that I've got to fit in during the week and it's also my mum's 90th birthday party so it will be a very busy week. Hopefully I'll get time to catch up with many of you at some time or other.

Best wishes,
Martyn

BACK IN CHENGDU FOR SUMMER SUN? –
2nd July 2014

I landed in the Chengdu mist on Monday of last week after a busy, but enjoyable, 9 days in the UK. It was really good to meet many of you, get to my mother's 90th birthday party, play a couple of games of golf (very rusty!!) and have the first BBQ of the year. My mother's (and her twin sister, Auntie Phyl) joint 90th birthday party spread over two days was a major event bringing together many old friends and lots of relatives, some of which I didn't know I had!! My brother Simon and his wife Emma really did a wonderful job organising and hosting the whole thing. Luckily I was able to get away before the clearing up began, having the excuse of catching the flight back to China. It was obviously a very sociable few days since I put on about 5 pounds in weight and lost many more from my bank account!!

So, what's been happening in the last few weeks? As far as my businesses are concerned, we seem to be making slow but steady progress since both our Chinese customers are experiencing a reduction in volume from what they planned. When asked, they both blame it on what I would describe as financial constipation. Not really a technical term but quite apt since their customers are the hospitals and apparently they are not getting the funds flowing through to buy the MRI scanners at the rate they expected. Also, one of the customers is waiting for a new round of investment funding to be approved and currently has no cash to pay suppliers. This is my only customer for the smaller of my 2 factories so I have nowhere else to go to get money, therefore it is a daily fight to get cash. A couple of weeks ago I had less than £200 in the company bank account!! Today I need them to pay me the equivalent of £8,000 so that tomorrow (3rd July) I can pay the June wages for all my Chinese staff. However I'm hoping that next month the cash problem will reduced, only to be replaced with other issues no doubt. It is all this stuff that keeps doing business in China interesting, but often frustrating.

When I first came to China back in 2006 most of the Chinese, particularly the young, aspired to be like Westerners and so most of the advertising in magazines, on bill boards and on television showed good-looking Western men and women using whatever the product was and even speaking English with Chinese subtitles. Well over the years I have noticed the advertising gradually change. For one thing there's much more in every walk of life, from televisions on the Metro to the whole sides of buildings lit up with screens telling you what to buy. But perhaps more subtly the faces in the adverts have changed from out and out Westerner, through a phase of Asian with Western features (the nose and eyes are the giveaways!) to what now is predominantly Asian. Why? Well quite simply the Chinese now have a generation of very rich people experiencing a lifestyle of luxury comparable to anything in Hollywood. They have their own international film stars, designers and artists and so the new Chinese aspire to be like their successful country-men, which in some ways makes it seem more attainable. The other advantage is that no plastic surgery is required even though there is still mass marketing for cosmetic skin whitening products. What's the next stage? Maybe, fairly soon we'll see advertising in the West featuring good-looking Asians promoting the benefits of a yellow skin!!! What comes around goes around!!!

Although, as I predicted in my previous email, England's time in the World Cup was neither long nor happy, the Chinese are still following it all with interest. A couple of the girls in the office are now ardent followers of Germany (so no pay increase for them this year, bitter? moi? or should that be bitte?). I also had to endure dinner with a very smug guy from the USA last Sunday asking how the country that gave soccer to the world could not even win one game. Anyway at least Belgium have seen them off. The shops are still promoting soccer-associated stuff, and to be honest I have found the discount on World Cup beer difficult to resist, if only Cadbury would do some promotional event I would be in heaven! So I guess it's now down to following

Andy Murray (of the United Kingdom) for success at Wimbledon.

Wishing you all a great summer as the Chengdu thermometer heads toward 40 degrees C,
Ma Ding

BAMBOO EVERYWHERE!! – 21st July 2014

Over the years I've travelled in many Chinese cars and just about every vehicle has had seat covers fitted. At first I thought this was only to do with allowing the air to circulate more freely because many of these covers were made of bamboo or bamboo with some fabric covering. I'm still not sure, but Mr Slow has a full set, including head-rest covers installed. Now his car's covers are bamboo with some beige fabric covering and it feels as though you are sitting on a pile of twigs (which is probably true). The big problem is that the beige fabric fibres seem to come away easily and migrate into the seat and upper thigh area of my black work trousers. So after about two weeks the front and back of my trousers are a different colour and therefore have to be cleaned on a very regular basis. It's all right for Mr Slow, he wears beige-coloured trousers which look as though they were last cleaned in 2003! I'm thinking of becoming a club member of the local dry cleaning shop!

The other aspect of all this is that most cars in China, although having a completely shot engine and badly battered body work, will have pristine seats once the covers are removed. Whether this enhances the sale value, I'm not sure, but I remember when buying a second-hand car always checking to see whether the driver's seat was worn in relation to the supposed mileage on the car. In China you'll never know!!!

So I recently attended a meeting with the British Chamber of Commerce to discuss some of the key issues that small/medium-sized businesses based in South West China are faced with at the moment. This meeting was timed to allow the main points to be raised with the mayor of Chengdu in a few weeks' time. So I spoke about problems with local bank/finance support for small companies and also transport and pollution issues. The guy next to me, who is involved in placing British interns into roles in the region, had a completely different problem. Because these interns don't get paid he tries to place them with an accommodating Chinese family who will get a bit of rent in return for a room and food. However, he is having trouble finding sufficient accommodation with 'sit-down' Western loos; there are too many 'squatters', he said. This was actually a breakfast meeting, so we ended up discussing the merits and issues of 'squatters verses sitters' whilst eating our croissants!! I'm not sure that I would be comfortable complaining to the mayor of a 17 million population city that not enough of his toilets conform to the sensitive Western bottom requirements!! What can he really do about it anyway?

The other Friday, our Chinese production engineer, Robert, and I had to visit a supplier near the city of Yibin, some 300km south of Chengdu. Unfortunately it was decided that the best way to get there was to take the regular coach service which was significantly cheaper than using a hire car with driver, and also much quicker than the old train. There is a real contrast between the high-speed trains which get up to 300km/hour (nearly 200mph) and the normal trains which rattle along at about 40mph, stopping at every station. Also I was told that it would be worth visiting the Bamboo Sea forest park about 80km to the west of Yibin. So combining a work visit with a bit of sightseeing. No problems? Not likely, this is China! So at about 8.30am we duly turned up at the coach station, not far from my apartment, expecting a 3-hour journey in the air-conditioned luxury coach. Well, we were all on board for the 9.00am departure but the timetable had many coaches departing at about the same time and one of these decided to break down in the narrow exit. So there were about 15 coaches all wedged around the exit hooting and tooting, but nothing moved. After about 20 minutes of waiting for something to happen, several frustrated coach drivers got out and decided to push the offending vehicle out of the way. Having done that there was a big rush to get back on board and barge a way out. The police then decided to get involved to ensure that normal road traffic could flow reasonably whilst a stream of coaches wanted to get out of the coach station. As usual the police made matters worse! So about an hour late we finally had travelled the 100 yards to get out. Then there were other traffic problems and hold-ups, finally a taxi from Yibin coach station to the supplier's factory and so we eventually arrived mid-afternoon about 2 hours later than planned.

After the meetings the supplier kindly provided a car to take us to a town about 20km from the Bamboo Sea Park. Apparently we could then take an 'unofficial' taxi to the cheap hotel we had booked inside the park, and also buy a return coach ticket direct to Chengdu without having to stop again at Yibin. The plan being to visit the park on the Saturday morning and early afternoon, then get the 4.15pm coach arriving back in Chengdu at about 7.30pm. Well the first minor problem was that there were no seats available on the coach going back to Chengdu. We did get a local driver quite easily, who not only delivered us to the hotel but also offered for a reasonable sum, (reasonable for him!!) to take us around the park's best sights the next day. He would also keep checking up on the return tickets and had a contact who might be able to help. It has to be said that by now I was getting slightly concerned that plans were getting ever so slightly out of control. My hotel room at £26 was interesting in that it was open plan. Yes, the bed, toilet, shower and basin were all in the same open area with only the basin being located behind a pillar providing any privacy. Just as well I wasn't sharing. That evening we dined at an eatery (restaurant would be too good a word) recommended by the driver, feasting on bamboo eggs, bamboo stomach and bamboo flesh. Not as bad as it sounds and washed down with, you've guessed it, bamboo-based alcohol stuff.

Particularly appetising bamboo food.

On my way down to breakfast the next morning, as I was descending the stairs at the end of a corridor of guest rooms, I noticed that a few yards up the corridor there appeared at first sight to be a huge spider-type thing moving across the carpet. My first thought was that it looked like a tarantula. It then disappeared into the door recess of a guestroom and I heard some knocking on the door!!! Your fearless adventurer moved in to investigate. What I actually found was a medium-sized crab banging its shell on the bottom of the door and when it noticed me it turned round to face me and brought its claws up to scare me off. This hotel is probably about 1000 miles from the nearest sea so I could only think that 'crabby' had done a Ronnie Biggs and escaped from the kitchen pot. I did take a bit of video to give proof of this event to any doubters out there.

After a pretty grim breakfast we did indeed visit some very scenic areas: waterfalls, lakes and bamboo forest areas with the tree tops waving in the wind like a sea. One particular location was made famous in the film *Crouching Tiger, Hidden Dragon* ... a classic if ever there was one!!! Unfortunately the driver told us that there were still no tickets available for the return coach to Chengdu, so he suggested that he would take us to the town where he picked us up, we could then get a taxi back to Yibin and there were coaches every hour or two to Chengdu. Nothing to worry about then?? So working backwards we needed to leave the park at about 1.00pm. Actually the day was becoming very hot so I was pleased to get away earlier than originally planned. On the first part of the journey the driver informed us that instead of taking a taxi he had a mate who would take us the 50km to Yibin for a reasonable sum (about £15). This seemed to be more convenient so he dropped us at his mate's place who was already waiting in his car eager to get the money. This chap was actually a policeman but didn't seem to drive any better than the average Chinese driver, i.e. scary! After about 10 minutes this chap then said that he had a friend in Yibin who, if he could get 4 people in his car, would take us to Chengdu. Again this seemed to be a very convenient option for only £5 more than the coach fare. A few phone calls later it was all arranged and we were dropped off next to a brand new white Citroen. There was one other passenger already in the car and we set off to pick up another before hitting the road back to Chengdu. It turned out to be a smooth, quick journey and I was dropped off at my apartment building at about 5.30pm. Flexible Chinese transport at its best with loads of people willing to work to get some tax-free cash!! A win-win all round.

This week the temperature has been in the mid-30s and in the middle of the factory it feels a lot worse since the ceiling fans are just moving hot air around. I have therefore made an executive decision that our employees can have an ice cream 3 days a week and a cold drink every day. Obviously it's only fair to offer this benefit to our office workers as well (including myself!!).

I trust you are still enjoying the wonderful British summer,
Ma 'the crab chaser' Ding

DOGGY STORY – August 11th 2014

One of the problems of now being able to speak a bit of Chinese is that it has made me more confident in certain situations. For example last week I was out for an evening walk after sitting in the office all day and coming towards me was a lady walking her dog. Nothing strange in that, you think. But this terrier-type dog had bright pink long hairy ears and also sported a green, yellow and pink tail. I've been out and about several times and seen some oddly coloured dogs, but not had my camera to hand, so this time I thought I must take a photo. As I got my camera out I realised that the only way to do this was to stop the lady and ask her in my best Mandarin if I could photograph her colourful doggy. Although I made the excuse that the photo was for my daughter who thinks that the way Chinese dog owners dye the dog's hair is really interesting and beautiful, I actually think she realised that I thought the dog looked very odd. Anyway I thanked her and I did get the pictures.

A tail to die for.

In mid-July my apartment complex filled up the outdoor swimming pool and it is open from 10.30 in the morning until 9.30 at night. I thought I would be tempted to use it as the temperature is very high at the moment, but the pool seems to be occupied by screaming children most of the time. Now

241

my previous experience of Chinese swimming pools has been mixed, from the early days in Liuzhou where the hotel pool was huge and hardly ever used, but everyone had to wear a bathing cap, to the pool in my apartment complex in Hangzhou which seemed to have a green tinge possibly due to all the spitting going on. Here investigation showed that on a Saturday and Sunday morning before 11.00am the pool had very few users, and because I didn't want to be pointed at by children saying things like 'look Daddy there's a strange very white flabby foreigner' I decided to try for a quick dip last Sunday morning. So with an old pair of shorts to be used as my 'swimmers' I made my way to the pool enclosure, which is well hidden behind fences, trees and shrubs and at this time seemed nice and quiet. I entered to find that not only was the pool empty of children, it was also empty of water! No I didn't get in and do a few circuits in the fresh air, I beat a hasty retreat, hoping no-one had spotted this foreigner going for a swim without water. I'm told there was a leak that needs to be fixed and it should be filled up again by next weekend.

Back to one of my regular China subjects; driving. You probably heard about the recent bus crash which claimed 44 lives, all because some impatient driver tried to overtake the bus and came face to face with oncoming traffic and so forced the bus into the bridge side-rail which gave way, allowing the bus to topple off the bridge. This impatience is evident in many walks of life, from queuing (or lack of) at bus stops, for cinema tickets, preparing to get off the plane before it's landed and even for the horrible lunch in the staff canteen. Even if there is no gap, someone will eventually push in and try to get there earlier. I know we Brits have a queuing and fair-minded mentality but the implications of this impatience are never really thought through. As we were driving home the other day there was obviously a problem ahead because just after getting through the toll booth the traffic came to a stop. Six lanes trying at first to get into two, then after we eventually got onto the expressway itself it was back to four normal lanes plus the hard shoulder, which the

Chinese term the 'emergency lane'. Well obviously if I'm Chinese and not getting to where I want to go quickly enough, then I have an emergency so I can justify using the emergency lane. This lane then became used by a steady stream of impatient drivers, eventually coming to a stop as it too backed up. Then the emergency vehicle sirens were heard behind us but they were obviously not able to progress since the full width of the road was now blocked. So we just sat there, moving very occasionally, hampered by people constantly changing lanes, forcing a gap and sometimes having a small bump which just compounded the problem. There is no real lane discipline in China and no rule about overtaking on the outside as we have. So it's just chaos, even the lane markings are ignored. Four normal lanes plus the emergency lane soon became seven lanes of traffic, although in reality it was just a mass of vehicles. When, over an hour later, we got to where the problem was, a couple of scrunched vans, there had to my knowledge been another two accidents and probably many more due to the Chinese attitude to queuing. It's no wonder that China has the reputation of having the worst traffic jams and road deaths of anywhere in the world. Around 200,000 killed on the roads each year. I'm told that the worst traffic jam (recorded so far in China) was apparently 80kms long and took 4 days to clear.

Back to seasonal stuff!! The mangos and pineapples are gradually disappearing and have been replaced by lots of big black grapes, various types of melons and walnuts. But the walnuts are not as we know them . . . they still remain in their green fleshy shell. In Britain we very rarely see a walnut in its natural state, it's either been stripped of its outer coating revealing the nut we know or even more often now supplied ready de-shelled. We are getting increasingly lazy and possibly the next generation will no longer know how a walnut exists in the wild, so that when we tell them about the walnuts being dug up, a bit like potatoes, they won't know whether it's a porky or not!!! It also seems to be the season for the automatic wobble board. At least 2 shopping plazas that I visited recently had the central walk area devoted to exhibiting massage chairs and these wobble board things, best described as a large step about 6 inches off the ground which uses an electric motor to wobble in each and every direction. They had about 15 of these things in one place for any passer-by to try out. I have got some lovely video of very wobbly people. There was one old man in his vest, shorts and sandals who was on one of these things and it actually seemed quite frightening. For the technical amongst you I think the board was moving at his body's natural frequency which effectively meant that if the board moved an inch certain parts of his body were moving much, much more. It was quite funny to watch his whole body look like a huge lump of jelly shaking more and more with every passing second. However after not too long he began to look very scared and managed to get off before he was thrown off. Even the slimmest of people seemed to have plenty of bits wobbling away!!! I was not persuaded to have a go myself, I think I will stick to the fresh air swimming!!

I understand that the few weeks of wonderful UK weather has given way to storms from hurricane Ernie (or some other name). I hope it gets better soon.

Best regards,
Wobbly Mart

THE NOISES OF SUMMER!! –
September 10th 2014

The weather has been pretty hot and sticky recently with evening rainstorms that usually leave the mornings clear for a couple of hours before the fug and humidity build up again. This means that the air-conditioning systems are all working full blast a lot of the time and even the most miserly of taxi drivers is using their air con as opposed to opening all the windows to save a little money. However there is a downside to this as I discovered the other day when travelling back from the city centre after some meeting. I hailed the taxi in the tried and tested way; extending my arm and wildly flapping my hand at the wrist. I got into this cool but grubby taxi, told matey where I wanted to go and then sat back as we proceeded south to my apartment. After about 5 minutes the taxi driver started hawking. This happens in taxis quite regularly when we are stopped at traffic lights or in a jam and then the driver casually opens his door and spits on the road. But no, not this time, our careful driver did not want to risk his car getting warm, having spent money getting it cool, so he picked up a smallish receptacle from somewhere near the driver's door and let his spit flow. Charming, an in-car spittoon!! Whatever will they think of next? I had to suffer this on and off for the next 20 minutes. I'll try to take the metro as much as possible in future!

The fashion for putting transfers on cars to make them stand out from the norm has taken off in China. I remember the days of going to Halfords to buy some 'go faster' stripes for some old car. Again if you are very rich in China you can have any colour car you want and I've taken quite a few photos of some really expensive cars completely spoiled by a very gaudy paint job. I'll bore some of you later with the pix when I next get home. However coming back to the 'go faster' stripes and transfers: we were on our way back home on the expressway the other day when this throaty black Honda tried to overtake us on the inside (is that like under-taking? Given that it gets very dangerous) we noticed some thick yellow stripes down the side with the word NAMOTOM in between the stripes. Dean (my Production Manager) and I looked at each other as if to say 'what's all that about?' The traffic was quite heavy so this Honda was getting ahead of us for a bit and then would fall back alongside as we were puzzling over this word. Finally the penny dropped. The garage, or the individual, had put the transfer on back to front: it should have said 'motoman'!! I suppose it's an easy mistake to make if you just don't understand the language. I would have the same problem if a string of Chinese characters were back to front. We did see another inverted transfer job a few days later . . . YAWD3392!! (The font was a bit different).

So, you're a stinking rich Chinese guy with a fancy car and a rare (and strangely coloured) dog. What do you need now to show you've made it? A piano of course!! There are now over 50 million pianos in China and recently because of a particularly talented Chinese pianist they are selling like hot cakes. This chap called Lamg Lang has appealed to lots of younger Chinese in much the same way that Nigel Kennedy did with his fiddling in the UK a few years back. So now there are many millions of Chinese children studying the piano constantly so as to show off to their parents' friends and relatives. There are at least 2 pianos bashing away in my apartment complex on a regular basis. As ever the Chinese will persevere and technically many of these children will be extremely good, however I am told that for the vast majority their ability to interpret the music will be limited. Not that I have the ability to tell the difference.

One of the most interesting sights most evenings when walking around is finding large groups of older Chinese people out dancing. They will find a paved area and they will regularly practice their moves. It gets them out of their cramped apartments and gives them some exercise which has got to be a good thing. However, what you now find is that there are sometimes competing groups of dancers all dancing in the same area, this is probably because there are increasing numbers of older people in China (like most countries) and they are being persuaded to look after themselves and do more exercise. So now you get the 'battle of the music machines' with each group turning up the volume so that their members can hear their music clearly and not get confused with the rhythm from the adjacent group. Whereas previously a group could bring a small cassette player and hear their music, now they seem to be bringing large ghettoblasters to out-do each other. Unfortunately the local government are getting involved and stopping the music and therefore the dancing, which is a real shame. OK, it's loud music but it's a lot better than some of the noises that are pretty constant in China, not least the hooting of taxis and the whip cracking spinning top thing that I told you about a few weeks ago. Hopefully they will find a happy compromise.

I should be back for just over a week in mid-October, so I look forward to seeing some of you then.

Best wishes,
Ma Ding

BACK AGAIN FOR AUTUMN –
October 27th 2014

The few days I spent in England seemed to go so quickly and unfortunately I didn't get time to see everyone I wanted to. What with travelling to Exmouth, Norfolk, London, Surrey, Cambridge and Salisbury, I felt that I was rarely at home. Never mind, Christmas is coming, and I will get back for a week and make sure I spend most of it at home. Julie came back to Chengdu with me for a few days. The highlight of course was visiting the Pandas; luckily the weather was good, and we arrived early so it wasn't too busy. Also, for the first time in all Julie's visits to China she declared the food to be OK, the wine passable and it didn't rain until the day she left!!

Business in China has slowed down a lot, partly due to the new President's anti-corruption drive. The 'grease' that ensured the flow of orders and supplies has begun to be removed from the system and so the whole thing feels a bit constipated. So although there is a huge market potential for the products we manufacture and supply, we currently need a huge dose of laxative to free up the orders. I'm told it should free up a bit in the next 2 months, which hopefully will coincide with the visit of our Main Board of Directors in December!

Lots of banging and raised voices from outside my apartment block the other Saturday morning waking me up earlier than I hoped. Going down later in the morning I noticed a wine dispenser had been installed in the lobby area. So just like the normal vending machines you see around various places which sell cans of Coke, etc, this thing was selling bottles of wine. Someone obviously thought that the type of residents in this place couldn't be bothered to walk a couple of hundred yards to the supermarket or off-license but could pop down any time of day or night in their pyjamas to buy a bottle of Chateau le Dragon. When I looked more closely at the selection of 6 bottles, they ranged from a basic French white at £11 to a French red at, would you believe, £94. How they keep an expensive bottle of wine at the right temperature when outside it can be anywhere between 5 to 40 degrees I don't know? Will the Chinese drinker taste the difference? Probably not. Will he or she care? Certainly not. All very convenient.

Best vintage French wines from £11-£94.

Talking of convenient, I was walking towards the market the other Saturday and passed a large apartment block outside which a grubby van with a big cage on the back was parked. There was a gaggle of locals around it, so I slowed down to investigate. It was a choose-your-own-live-chicken supplier. The customer would have a good look, point and say, "I want that one," whereupon the van guy would open the cage door, pull out the selected bird, hang it upside down and deftly slit its throat. He then handed it to a lady, possibly his wife, who would proceed to pluck it, put it in a bag and give it to the customer in exchange for some notes. I carried on to do my shopping, and on passing the same spot on the way back about an hour later all I saw was a pool of blood and big pile of feathers. A couple of women soon appeared to scoop the feathers into a big sack, probably to make pillows or dusters. Everything gets eaten or used in China!!

It was a National Holiday at the beginning of October and we had a few days off. Unfortunately, just like Chinese New Year there are so many people travelling it is virtually impossible to get transport or hotels at a reasonable price. My colleague Dean decided to spend 3 days in Beijing seeing the sights, whereas I decided to stay in Chengdu and try to fit in a couple of local visits, there and back in a day. I was told that about a 90-minute bus ride to the south of the city was a pretty old town called Huanglongxi. I went to the local bus station the day before to get the ticket and because it was holiday season the place was swarming with people all pushing and shoving to get to the front of the queue. I've learned to get a bit 'Chinese' with this process now and give as good as I get in queues. Luckily I've got bony elbows! Again the problem is that, although it was possible to buy the ticket to get to the place (only £2.60), you could only buy the return ticket once you arrived at Huanglongxi. Anyway the next day I set off for the visit. The coach left on time and seemed to be making good progress but once we got within about 2 miles of the place the roads just clogged up with cars, buses and bikes. The area around this town is a large grape growing region, so all around were stalls selling lots of eating grapes of various colours, which was interesting. However it took nearly an hour to cover the last few miles and arrive at the bus station. Then I had to queue for a return ticket, and because it was holiday season there were no specified return coach times, I just got given my ticket and told when I wanted to go back to Chengdu I would just have to wait for the next coach, which were supposed to run every 20 minutes.

Then I set off with the throng to find the 'pretty old town'. It was very easy to find the way because many thousands were all going in the same direction. It felt a lot like leaving a stadium or theatre at the end of an event, you can only go with the flow. The old town was full of narrow alleys, little shops, water wheels driven by the stream that ran along the main street and lots of flowers. But because of so many people, it was very noisy, extremely smelly with the local foods and impossible to appreciate. It didn't take me too long to lose the will to live. Unfortunately more and more people were arriving, and it was very difficult to make my way out against the tide. I stopped to buy an ice cream, gathered my strength and then forced my way out. Again queuing for the coach home was a nightmare since there were many different queues all going to different places, crossing each other or merging at various places. However, I eventually managed to get on a coach back to Chengdu and arrived at my apartment in a fairly exasperated state. I quickly tore up the list of other places I had intended to visit in the following couple of days.

I expect you are all preparing for winter after what I hear has been an excellent summer. Hopefully I'll get to see many of you when I am back at Christmas.

Best wishes,
Ma Ding

WEATHER CONTROL – 12th November 2014

If you've been following the news over the last few days you will probably have seen that China is hosting a meeting of the APEC (Asia Pacific Economic Community) leaders in Beijing. These are the heads of the countries that border the Pacific and include President Obama, Putin, and Tony Abbot from Australia as well as many others. Yet again, as with the 2008 Olympics, China is keen to show Beijing in the very best of circumstances.

So although a few days ago the smog was so bad that planes were being diverted, schools were closed and many people stayed indoors, for the period of the APEC meeting the air is clear and pollution levels better than most of the world's big cities. In fact, yesterday the Air Quality index was 46 (good) for Beijing but 265 (very unhealthy) for Shanghai; just over a week ago the index for Beijing was over 300, which is termed 'hazardous'. So how did the Chinese government achieve this improvement in the weather? On further investigation it seems that last week all construction activity came to a halt in and around the city, most factories have been told to close for 6 days with all employees having extra holidays and the clouds have been seeded to ensure there was some rainfall to clear the air. It won't be long before there will be no need for weather forecasts in China . . . what do you want? OK, we can arrange that!!!

An interesting development which has caused some amusement as we take our weary ride to and from work every day. The queues at the toll booths for entering and exiting the expressway have been lengthening as the number of cars on Chengdu's roads continuously increases. So some bright spark in Road Traffic Control has looked at other cities and decided that if ETC (electronic toll collection) is introduced, not only will it allow many cars to flow through without stopping, it will also save money on not having to man the booth. For example, the exit road off the expressway that we use in the evening has 3 booths and consequently 3 queues, at which our driver, Mr Slow, always manages to choose the slowest. The people in the booth hold a hand out, get given our blue plastic card (no payment is required because ours is a Chengdu registered car), push a button to raise the barrier and away we go. For a few days beforehand there seemed lots of notices in Chinese announcing the implementation of the new ETC system and then suddenly last week one of the 3 lanes became the ETC lane and chaos reigned.

Obviously in the first few days not many drivers had signed up to this new system so most of the traffic now had to form 2 queues instead of 3, stretching back a long way. Then other drivers who either had signed up for the ETC or just thought they should be allowed through this lane started to queue up in the ETC lane. Unfortunately it seemed to us that for every 4 or 5 drivers who had genuinely paid extra for this 'efficiency', there was at least one who entered the number plate detection area and was not registered, therefore the barrier stayed down. He was then of course stuck with lots of ETC registered drivers queued up behind him and no human being to sort out the problem because they had saved on employment. So with many people getting out of their cars, lots of shouting trying to get a line of twenty or more cars to back up, so the unregistered car could get out and try and force its way into one of the other lanes, it was all good fun. We were just sitting in our even longer queues waiting to go through. I'm sure that without this extra entertainment I would have been a very unhappy bunny. Since then, the powers that be seemed to have manned up for this 'man free' lane so that drivers who do get it wrong don't have to back up but get through virtually normally. So guess what? Now unregistered vehicles just use the ETC lane as a quicker way of getting through, saying, "Whoops I got in the wrong lane, please take my card as normal."

Consequently the whole system is back to normal with everyone using all 3 lanes and those who paid for the quick ETC lane feeling a mite upset. ETC (extra traffic chaos!).

Sometimes my Chinese just lets me down. The other Friday, Dean and I decided to try a different restaurant, a

Teppanyaki style place where the food is cooked in front of you. As you can probably guess from the name it is originally a Japanese style. Anyway we arrived and were seated along with about six others around this large stainless steel cooking area with a chef working away in the middle. Rather than order several different dishes I thought it would be easier to order the set menu for 2. Total of about £23 plus beers, which is probably on the high side of average in Chengdu. It all looked pretty good as trays of raw food came out ready for the Chef to cook.

The Chef was obviously cooking for the other punters at the same time, and it was quite fun to just watch the skill as each dish was prepared and delivered to whoever had ordered it. I have to say that I didn't know exactly what was going to be included in our set menu, but I made sure there was some steak, prawns and vegetables in there somewhere. Then our food started to be cooked and placed on plates in front of us ready to eat, which we did, nodding in the satisfied way you do at the freshness and taste. And so it continued, through pepper steak, prawns, sardines, mushrooms wrapped in beef, spicy squid rings, various vegetables, etc. until we both looked at each other and said, "I can't eat any more, let's tell them to stop," which I did, and then asked for the bill. And yes, you've guessed it, the bill was double what we expected, since the set menu for 2 was actually priced for 1, and we were 2. Certainly we felt that there was probably enough food for 4. As the idiot foreigner I did say the bill wasn't right and that we only expected to pay about £30 with the drinks. After a bit of discussion they relented and we walked out feeling very bloated but still with enough money to visit the local bar.

We seem to be getting a real variety of weather at the moment; if it's not raining then it's cold in the morning, sunny during the middle of the day and then gets pretty grotty in the evenings. I'm told it's the transition for a couple of weeks before winter kicks in. I must find out who I need to talk to so that we can get the weather improved. No doubt you have to pay someone at the 'weather control bureau' as well!

We've got the big, big bosses all coming out for the parent company's main board meeting on December 2nd. So I'm getting everything cleaned up ready and practising doffing my cap to the great and the good!!! However, I don't think I'll be able to get all the construction stopped and the factories closed so the air is clear in Chengdu for this bunch.

Best wishes,
Ma Ding

CHINA RULES – OK?? – December 6th 2014

All the big bosses from our parent company, Avingtrans PLC, were with us for most of last week. They were over in China to hold their board meeting and get a first-hand view of what was happening with their 3 businesses based in Chengdu. (I run 2 of them and the other one belongs to the Aerospace Division). As ever with people living in the rarefied atmosphere of the main board, they had no idea how to look after themselves. So I had to organise virtually every element of the transport, hotel rooms and all the food, (God forbid that they swallowed a piece of pig face or whatever). Another reason for coming over was to finally make a decision for the next phase of investment in our new factory. I say finally because although this next phase was originally planned for May/June time this year, events and the Board's own risk averse nature have conspired to delay it until now. So I had to make a positive pitch for the investment, even though in reality there is no option. Well, OK there is: either we carry on as we are, losing thousands of pounds each month because we don't have the equipment to do what is required, or we invest in the phase 2 equipment and become capable of sourcing cheaper local material, doing all the manufacturing and selling these big bits of metal at a profit. Simples!

The result? Well they agreed to the investment on the condition that . . . blah, blah, blah . . .

You may recall that I inherited the new factory as an empty shell and we have had to turn various concrete holes into passable offices, meeting rooms and toilets, and also get large new machines up and running in the factory area. That was at the beginning of the year and 10 months later some of the renowned Chinese quality has reared its ugly head. We bought lots of new furniture: desks, cabinets and tables in a very modern mid-grey wood grain finish. And 10 months later after the summer sun all the edging on the furniture has turned a putrid shade of green. We called the suppliers in to look at it. Initially the discussion seemed to be going along the lines of the dead parrot sketch from Monty Python. You know ... "Well sir that's just temporary, lovely colour, sir, we call it Sichuan grey," etc. etc. Eventually they did agree to replace the edging. Will the replacement last another 12 months? Who knows, this is China!

The other Friday I had to go to meet our major customer in Shenzhen so Dean, my deputy, who I hope will be in a position to take over from me in 6 months' time, went to a conference with lots of other potential local customers. This was a bash at a hotel about 2 hours west of the city which had been organised by the local manufacturing association. Apparently, there were over 300 people at this thing, representing 80 different companies, who were there for the Thursday afternoon, the evening banquet and the Friday until mid-afternoon. Dean, who was one of only about 3 other foreigners, unfortunately found himself being toasted many, many times during the course of the evening, luckily only full glasses of red wine rather than the horrible baijiu stuff. He survived to fight another day and for his perseverance the organisers gave everyone a going away gift; a reasonable-sized cardboard box. There wasn't the opportunity to open the box on the coach home so you can imagine Dean's dismay when, thinking he was going to get a new jacket or something useful, the contents turned out to be a box of recyclable bog rolls. (Toilet rolls made from recycled paper, not from old toilet rolls!) Well, I told him it's all good training for when you become the General Manager!! (Patronising sod that I am!)

I know I keep going on about the driving problems, the pavement parking, product quality and many other issues. It finally occurred to me that when you dig into these things there are lots of rules in China, it's just that nobody bothers to follow them because the police don't really enforce them. The only thing that generally gets any form of real police action is a murder or closing a city so that foreign dignitaries will see China in the best light. A complete contrast to the UK where if you even think of parking near a double yellow line some officious 'person' will rush out and slap a fine on your windscreen. In China even if a policeman is in the vicinity of

257

a transgression it is always possible he will turn a blind eye, given a small inducement!!

Talking of which, as you know the new President is really cracking down on anti-corruption in all sectors of Chinese life, including the many millions of employees in state-owned companies and government offices. It has come to light that some members of the anti-corruption force have now been accepting bribes to let the corrupt offenders off. So now I expect to hear that a new anti-anti-corruption force will be established to root out the corrupt anti-corruption officials. Nothing really changes, it just gets more confusing!!

The Chinese commercial Christmas sprang into life on the first day of December with most shop assistants and restaurant waitresses wearing red hats with white bobbles, lots of naff Christmas trees sprouting up all over the place and the shops playing Rudolf the Red xxxxxxx Nose Reindeer!! I now try to avoid shopping because the constant repeating music gets on my nerves so much. Bah Humbug!!!

Hopefully I will be back in a couple of weeks' time to spend Christmas at home and relax for a few days.

Best wishes,
Ma Ding (dong merrily on high!)

HAPPY NEW YEAR – 9th January 2015

Well after an eventful few days at home I'm back in the land of the fug for what I hope will be the final session. I say eventful few days since we did have a couple of dramas over the Christmas break: for those of you not living in Painswick the first drama occurred on the Tuesday before Christmas as I was under instruction from the boss to check that the dining room log fire was working properly, following the chimney being swept a couple of months earlier to clear it of birds' nests, etc. Having other stuff to get on with I dutifully lit the fire and went out to the garage only to hear Julie screaming for me a few minutes later. Yes, you've guessed it, the chimney caught fire and was roaring like a jet engine. Bucket of water on the fire but it was still well alight up the chimney and the thick metal tube running from the fire canopy up the chimney was glowing bright red. Panic mode set in, so we called 999 and also called our local firefighter, Andy, from across the road. Now Andy, having worked as a retained fire-fighter in Painswick for the last 10 years, had finally retired the week before. Luckily he hadn't forgotten all his training, so was able to come to our rescue and with the help of some squirty water bottles put the fire out. Just as well since the local fire appliance from Stroud (4 miles away) was having problems getting to us. I could hear the siren around the valley but no sign of the actual vehicle. Eventually, about 15 minutes later it did turn up, by which time everything was cooling down. At least they were able to do a thorough check of the house.

The second drama occurred on Christmas Eve as I returned home with a car full of senior people and suitcases. I had gone to Oxford in Julie's VW EOS (2 door coupe) to pick up my mother, Auntie Phyl and Auntie Joy, combined age 272!!! Unfortunately, as my mother was trying to manoeuvre herself out of the back seat of the car she slipped, so that her bum was trapped in the footwell. The seat was as far forward as I could get it but there was no easy way to pull or push her into a position to get out. I even tried a plank of wood from behind. The funny side of the situation was OK for about 15 minutes as we tried all sorts of twisting and pulling but it was getting cold. So for the second time in a couple of days we called for the local firefighter (still retired). Andy again came to the rescue and proceeded to use a very clever fireman's lift (page 37 of the manual) to extract my mother from the car. It's what we pay our taxes for!!! Thank you.

I have arrived back in China somewhat heavier than when I departed 10 days earlier. This is mainly due to Julie's excellent cooking and my lack of willpower when faced with English beer, chocolate opportunities in every room and many deserts with every meal. Luckily a return to boiled pig's face and spicy goose throat will soon get me back down to my fighting weight. Well, I don't seem to have missed much since I've been away. Our customers still don't have many orders to give us, so work is very quiet. The Chinese have blocked the G-mail system which is what we have been using until we get our new business computer up and running, so communications were difficult for a few days until we all moved to a new system. Hopefully work will begin to pick up after Chinese New Year which is mid-February this year. The year of the sheep (or goat) is on offer this year. It is actually my year, that is to say that I was born in the year of the Sheep, so given that there are 12 animals, I will be some multiple of 12 years old this year. No prizes for guessing it's not 48 (who said 72??).

Being ultra-observant I have noticed that the local supermarket, Carrefour, has a very flexible pricing arrangement on certain products. I often alternate between Carrefour (very local) and Auchan (about 20 mins walk) to buy my breakfast cereal, knowing that prices for the same products are often very different in each store. However, I have now realised that Carrefour actually puts the price of some products up by 15% at the weekend. It then comes back down on the Monday. Is this something unique to French supermarkets in China, or is it more widespread? Have Tesco been doing something similar? We need to know!!

I had to endure the bank again this morning to send some money back to the UK. It is something I do every 2-3 months and it entails taking loads of documents into the bank (HSBC Chengdu) and waiting over an hour whilst they go through everything several times, take countless copies and cross-check everything with a supervisor. Eventually, when it was sorted, I decided it would be easier to take the metro out towards the factory and then have the driver meet me and take me the final 10 minutes' drive to my office. The metro takes about 40 minutes and cost 45p. However today for the first part of the journey I was unable to get a seat so just stood looking at the people. Sitting down just across from me were an old couple with their young grandson of about 18 months who was playing with a small toy bicycle. They were doing quite well controlling him until he obviously wanted to have a wee. Rapidly trousers were pulled down and a nappy was sourced from somewhere, but it was too late, little laddie proceeded to pee all over the place, splashing one of the unfortunate ladies sitting next to Grandma. Grandpa was doing his best to stem the flow but was also getting soaked. The puddle was moving towards me, so I quickly moved to another carriage. Not something you see on the London Underground, or is it?

I hope you are all sticking to your New Year resolutions. I was going to try the no-choccy in 2015 trick, but unfortunately I received many chocolate Christmas presents this year, which I have brought back to China with me. I feel it would be very rude not eat these presents that friends and relatives have so kindly given me. Perhaps 2016 is the year of no-choccy!!!

Best wishes to you all for 2015,
Ma Ding

FINE AND DANDY – 8th February 2015

February already and I've finished my Christmas choccy so feeling a bit lardy. The problem is that it's so bitterly cold at the moment that I don't feel like eating salads and other healthy fare. These two months are so depressing, and I see that the UK is much the same, weather wise, at the moment. It's not helped by very little work from both our customers, so the days go by really slowly. I did get a new 10-year contract agreed and signed with one of the customers, but currently they have very few orders, we are all hoping it picks up after Chinese New Year. The other customer is just being the worst of a mixture of German and Chinese trying to beat us up for lower prices. I have to say I'm in the mood for a fight on this one so it'll be interesting over the next few weeks when they want deliveries and I need a price that will give me a little bit of profit.

My full-time work will definitely finish at the end of April, which is also when the lease on my apartment expires. So now all I have to do is try to negotiate a bit of part-time work to keep me busy whilst I drift into semi-retirement. So I'm really looking forward to catching up with friends and family, some clean air, Julie's cooking, British beer with some taste and some variable golf!!

We had a big Burns Night bash the other Saturday organised by the local British Chamber of Commerce in conjunction with the Chengdu Whisky Tasting club! This was quite a formal event with about 100 people shipped in coaches to one of the 'resorts' on the outskirts of the city. This particular resort is called the Diamond Bay Club, about 40 minutes' drive from the centre, and consisted of some very impressive mansions, apartments, leisure facilities and a fancy hotel all surrounding a large lake with landscaped hills. This is one of several resort areas springing up in China to cater for the newly wealthy who want to get away from the city at the weekend. The only downside I could see as we arrived in the coach, was the really awful air quality, probably not helped by what looked to be a cement factory on the hillside behind the lake. Anyway, to the event itself. A mixture of ex-pats and Chinese with several Scots wearing their full national dress (take the word in both senses). The haggis had been flown in especially for the occasion and the menu was the traditional Burns Night stuff. Dean, my work colleague, and I bought a couple of tartan bow ties for the occasion to wear with our dark suits, very fetching! There was the usual reciting of Rabbie Burns poems, which could have been in Chinese for all that anyone understood, and also some singing of Auld Lang Syne. One of the interesting things was that two of the Chinese ladies on our table just wouldn't eat the haggis, thinking it had all sorts of horrible stuff in it. These are the same people who, when given a preference, will regularly eat goose throat, chicken feet, various insects and fish stomach and eyes, compared to which haggis is pretty normal. There really is no accounting for taste. A good night was had by all with plenty of whisky and wine available on each table.

Here's a first. You will recall yours truly being a bit put out having to walk in the gutters due to cars either parking or using the pavements as another lane. Well, for the first time in all my years in China I saw a policeman walking down a row of cars parked on the pavement, taking down the numbers. Just like you can see in any British town any day of the week when cars are breaking our parking regulations.

Priority pavement car parking.

However I then got to thinking about what said policeman is going to do with his list of maybe 20-30 vehicles. I suppose he has 4 options: firstly, he could just do nothing. Secondly, he could give the list to a colleague at the local nick. Thirdly (and I think we are getting into the more likely scenarios), he will probably do a filter exercise on the list after checking out the vehicle owners, just to make sure none of his colleagues, bosses or government chiefs are going to be fined, since that would be the end of his career, and then put the reduced list through the official fining system. Lastly, and probably the one with the least risk and giving him some reward, he could approach those on the shortlist personally to offer them a reduced penalty in cash or kind. We will never know but my money's on the latter.

In the same area as the policeman was doing his 'duty' which is just around the corner from my place, they have been replacing all the drain covers in the gutters. Only the odd thing is that all the drains have been raised up by about 10cm (4 inches in old money). These are smallish 2-way roads, although they can be 3-way plus both pavements on occasion, and the drains are opposite each other, so now there is a narrowing effect every 20-30 yards on these roads. This has led to great fun and games, as drivers are swerving in and out to avoid bursting their tyres, but also lots of stopping and starting as cars come at you nearly head-on. One of these is a road we use every day returning from work and I have been expecting road works to start as if they are going to resurface the road, however nothing has happened now for 5 weeks. Even if they raised the road to level of the drains there would be virtually no kerb so I'm not sure what is going on. One thing is for certain, unless there is a pretty strong flood in the near future, not one drop of water will ever be going into these drains.

Chinese New Year is now imminent and the whole country is slowing down. It could be argued that my business can't get much slower, however the material we have been waiting for from the UK has now been sitting in the port at Shanghai for over 3 weeks. We are told that this is all due to congestion as companies try to ship and receive goods prior to the holiday. As ever the shops are now full of lots of red stuff including sheep and goats since it is the year of the Goat next year. Also lots of gaudy lights flashing on and off outside buildings and on the trees, together with many red lanterns. We will have our company Chinese New Year bash later this week. It will be the normal old thing of an OKish meal at some local restaurant with the workforce relentless in their efforts to get the foreigners (Dean and I) drunk then probably on to a Karaoke bar for some horrendous warbling! Yes, I'm really looking forward to it!!!!

I hope you're all keeping fit and well,
Best wishes for the new year of the Goat,
Martyn

IS IT A GOAT OR A SHEEP? –
February 26th 2015

Well that's got that over with for another year. The year of the Sheep, Goat, Ram, Lamb or Ewe has arrived. The single Chinese word 'Yang' covers all of the above, yet in English we don't have an equivalent, so we have a choice of what year it is. The year of the Sheep seems the most common, however I'm all for wishing Ewe a Happy New Year!!! This year the government had banned fireworks from the large city centres and so, for the first time, there wasn't even one cracker let off during the holiday period. Very quiet and boring. In fact there were loads of police all around the city ensuring that people behaved themselves. I decided to stay in Chengdu, but although there are many interesting places in China I still want to visit, during the Chinese New Year holiday the prices of all the flights go up and the hotels charge triple the normal rate for a room. Not only that, even if the cost wasn't an issue, the places I want to visit would just be totally packed with Chinese visitors pushing, shouting and spitting. So if you go travelling at Chinese New Year you pay a fortune for the least pleasant experience. I'll try to take a couple of long weekends to visit places like the Three Gorges Dam, the Stone Forest and Zi Gong Dinosaur Park before I return to the UK.

I was invited to my friends Mark and Scarlet's home for the traditional Chinese New Year's Eve family meal. (Mark and Scarlet taught me Chinese in 2008-9 when they lived in Stroud, Goucestershire). There were about eight of us and we ate the traditional Jaozi (dumplings) with some assorted meats. Luckily none of the dreaded baijiu liqueur was available, just beer and red wine. The next day I went to the Crowne Plaza hotel, where my mate William is the General Manager, and they had the traditional lion dancing show for the guests. Not real lions, a bit like our pantomime horse, two blokes for each lion costume, however they are very elaborate and skillfully done. Although I had seen this a few times before, there is always something a bit different and this

The lion ready to roar.

time the lions had to leap up and grab what looked like a grotty lettuce hung from the ceiling. Apparently it's supposed to symbolise a good supply of food for the coming year, hopefully not just boring salads. It might have been better if there had been a pork chop hanging down but I guess that would just quickly get nicked!

On the Monday I did book a trip to the (world famous) Stone Elephant Lake, a park about one hour southwest of Chengdu. As ever it was relatively easy to book the bus to the place, but you can only get the return ticket when you arrive at the destination. This is one of the most frustrating things about travel in China, there is no concept of a return ticket. For flights and the high-speed trains you can book the separate ticket back at the same time as the outbound ticket, but for buses and coaches, unless it's a guided tour, you have to worry about the return when you get to the destination. Unfortunately on the Monday it was raining so the whole thing was pretty miserable. OK, there were a few stone elephants scattered around and obviously a lake, but most of the flowers which were supposed to be quite stunning were not yet open. A few tulips and daffs to brighten up the damp green scenery. Luckily because of the weather there weren't too many visitors, so it ended up as a quiet walk around a lake, up and down a few wooded hills and a bowl of spicy noodles under my umbrella. The journey back was not too bad; a small bus to the next biggest town and then a 50-minute wait for the main coach back to Chengdu. On one of the other days I decided to go to IKEA to get some more choccy, however when I got there I couldn't get in since they had erected lots of barriers to manage the queues of hundreds (maybe thousands) of Chinese all wanting to spend a few hours walking around the shop. It was just like a bad day queuing to get into a famous tourist attraction or the best Disneyland ride. The notice at the entry to the barriers stated that entry to the store was restricted due to too many shoppers. As you know I am not the most patient individual sometimes so I wasn't going to wait just to pop in through the exit to buy some choccy. I certainly didn't want to tour the shop, so I decided to return just before closing time (10.00pm). Even then it was pretty busy, but at least I had stocked up on my vital supplies!

I know that most of you were probably completely riveted by the story of the raised drains and lack of gutters on the roads near my apartment, so I can now give you the next instalment ... Just before Chinese New Year the roads with the raised drains were resurfaced. As I explained in the last email the drains were about 3-4 inches above the road surface and so the resurfacing brought the new road up to the level of the drains. That sounds OK even though it seems an enormous amount of tarmac to make the roads look better. However, the result is that the pavements in most places are now, at best, on the same level as the road surface and in very many places significantly lower than the road. So

268

yet again the drains are useless since the rain just flows onto the pavements. (I have lots of photographic evidence of this for anyone who thinks that roadworks cannot be that daft). Now thinking about this I have decided that there must be another explanation or motive for this situation. I've come up with two options: firstly, now the pavements and roads are at about the same level it is clear that with a few extra markings the pavements now become a couple of additional lanes for traffic. Secondly, you may remember a story from my time in Changzhou when I got some office decoration improvements done and the simple job of painting the walls led to replacing the carpet tiles and subsequently repainting the skirting boards and finally touching up the walls, etc. So I think this could be another case of job creation. Having raised the road they now have to raise all the pavements, which will then result in changing all the gates and driveways. So, another job creation programme all paid by the government!!

Not much else to report. The work situation remains difficult. Material from the UK which we needed to work on urgently arrived in Shanghai on the 21st January and due to the Chinese New Year holiday has still yet to arrive at our factory some 5 weeks later (it normally takes about 10 days). So the customer is not a happy chappy. Also, for the first time in my career I have been unable to pay the staff wages on time. This was the payment of what is known as the 13th month, usually paid to the Chinese employees just before the New Year holidays so they can eat and drink themselves silly. However our customer didn't have enough money to pay what they owe us; consequently I couldn't pay my staff. Very frustrating. I hope this will get resolved in the next few days.

I'm now counting down the weeks and hope to see you all and breathe some clean air soon.

Best wishes,
Ma Ding

BACK HOME SOON – March 12th 2015

Although our new factory is still having problems with our major customer because of yet another reduction in their forecast volume, I have arranged to move to part-time working from the end of April. In effect this means that I will spend between one and two months at home supporting the business remotely with the odd phone call or Skype session and then have a couple of weeks in China ensuring the customer relationships and general business targets are on track. During this time I will be steadily handing over to my side-kick Dean. (We are known as Dean Martyn at the local bar, and although our drinking is similar to our namesake, our singing certainly isn't!) The new work arrangement is a bit like the jobs I was doing many years ago when I was based in the UK with responsibility for many overseas companies and so I would generally visit most of them every three months or so. The big difference this time is that I will not be working in between the overseas visits, hurrah!!! I'm hoping that this arrangement will last at least until the end of the year. So please sort out the weather for me as I will be back on May 1st.

A few months back I mentioned the local governments were trying to introduce controls on the many groups of older people who regularly dance in the open areas around most cities. This was because of the increased noise from the ghetto blasters trying to compete with other dancing groups and the traffic noise. Well not much has changed so the problem has been raised to the central government level, who are now introducing new laws which will only allow 12 types of dances and limit the noise levels. These Granny Dancers, as they are called, since they are mainly ladies of a certain vintage, are now potentially criminals if they don't follow the approved dances or if they turn the music up too loud. They only do this dancing to get out of the house and keep active so that they don't cause a burden on the health service. I also find it very interesting as I walk around the city passing these highly organised groups, sometimes of over

270

200 people, doing their dancing to mostly Western music. Very occasionally I've joined in, much to the amusement of all and sundry. In reality I'm not sure anything will change. It will be just like lots of other laws and rules in China, no-one will enforce it until lots of people start dying or it gets in the way of China promoting itself to the outside world.

Our new factory was broken into last week and a few items, including a welding machine, were stolen. The total value wasn't too great (a few hundred pounds) but the fear is that they could easily come back for another go. It seems that the quality of the window catches is so poor that with limited pushing the catch easily breaks off, allowing the windows to slide open. So, what about our other security arrangements, I hear you ask? Well, our fearsome guard dog remained fast asleep throughout the intrusion, as did the security guard, and the CCTV cameras, of which we have nine, positioned inside and outside the factory, were useless because the recording system has been broken for a few months and no-one has bothered to check it. This event really highlights the Chinese attitude to quality and not fixing something until after it's needed. So yet again we will introduce new rules and checks to overcome lack of common sense.

Earlier on in my time in China I could go to the local meat and veg market and get half a kilo of sliced pig's ears, a pig's nose and if I was feeling particularly adventurous even a pig's face. This pig's face was usually a flattened thing that was either dried out or squidgy depending on how it was going to be eaten. Time has moved on in China and although the local markets still sell these products, I have now discovered them at the French supermarket, all carefully packaged for the discerning consumer. Also in order to give them an up-market feel the packaging has English writing on it. I attach photos from the supermarket's deli section. I know that many 'fine' foods in the UK often have French-sounding names to make them sound better than they otherwise might be: for example, Chateaubriand (slab of beef), Duck à l'orange (fatty bird with sickly sauce) or Coq au vin (chicken bits swamped in stale wine). So it is similar with these pig's bits packaging

Pig's bits forever.

when the Chinese read the English. So to get the right effect please try to say out loud with a French (Inspector Clouseau) accent, 'nez de cochon preserve', 'les oreilles de cochon coupe' or 'visage de porc seche'. I bet that makes you want to try these delicacies, so please place your orders and I will bring the packets home for you to use at your next dinner parties!

The weather these last few days has been very summery indeed, the rainstorm last Wednesday really cleared the air and for once a steady breeze seems to be keeping the pollution at bay. I just hope it continues for a few more days. Although China has adopted many Western festivals, such as Christmas and Halloween, if there is a hint of a commercial opportunity, it is odd that so far Easter has not been exploited and is only celebrated by the Christian community. However, I suspect with the current slowdown in China it won't be long before the shops are full of chocolate eggs, and Easter bunnies of varying shapes and sizes are everywhere. Watch this space!

Wishing you all a very Happy Easter.

Your international pig's snout supplier,
Ma Ding

THE LAST POST (REALLY!) – 25th April 2015

A few months ago, I was invited by my American friend Brian to be part of a quiz team for the fortnightly quiz evenings at the local bar/restaurant. About 7-8 teams take part with a maximum of 6 people in each team. With me included, our team, called Yang Qi (which means 'cool and trendy' in Sichuanese) includes Brian, a general manager and pianist who is four years younger than me, two much younger Brits who are teachers, Parry, a Chinese lady in her 40s, and then either Parry's partner, Bob, another American or Gordon, yet another teacher, but from Ireland. Why, I hear you say, did they ask me, the least trendy of anyone, to join a team called cool and trendy?? Obviously a mistake, but I joined the team mid-way through the last year and we ended up coming second for the year, winning 'beer' vouchers with which we all had a good celebration meal in January. We think we've got a good blend of age mix, with different nationalities, however the new season of quizzes has just commenced and in the first quiz we were completely useless, coming second-last. We blamed this on the fact that many of the questions seemed to be very USA-orientated and our best player Gordon was unavailable. So last Tuesday we were prepared for another embarrassment but surprisingly we did rather well. A good mix of questions which allowed us all to partic-ipate, and Gordon was again absent. I have a knack of coming up with the answers to some of the odd questions that no-one would expect me to know. For example, I recently answered a question about the pop group One Direction and correctly guessed that an odd quote was by Britney Spears, so apart from being the one they look to for historical facts about the UK (for example, who was the Queen's paternal grandmother?) I also manage to guess some of the weird ones. Goodness knows where I've picked up so much useless information which I didn't know I knew until asked. If only I could remember the things that really matter!!

Anyway, it's all good fun and last Friday the team plus some others decided to go for a typical meal in the Tibetan district of the city. 'Velly interesting' is the phrase that comes to mind. The setting was quite rustic; a big, long wooden bench table and hard chairs with lots of sombre-coloured wall coverings and waitresses dressed in Tibetan costume complemented by cow-bell background music and other occupants talking very loudly. The available drink was hot, sour yak's milk and most of the dishes were a variation of meat bits (yak or cow) with various potato or pancake things. I was told that the Tibetan vegetables were not good, so we didn't order any. However, yet another new experience and generally quite rowdy once the meal got underway.

Banking in China, what a farce!! I know some of you will remember some of my other banking stories but last week I had another 'this can't be real' event. Every three months or so I go to the HSBC branch in Chengdu and suffer a fairly torturous hour where lots of forms are filled in, photocopies of all my documents are taken (yet again) and computers checked and double checked. Then, and only then, can some local currency (Rmb) be transferred from my Chengdu current account to pounds in my Chengdu-based multi-currency account. I can then go home and by means of modern internet banking (if the internet is working), transfer these pounds in China to my HSBC account in Cheltenham. I have successfully done this for the last 18 months and last Wednesday hoped to do the same thing again. Now I have to say that when I first came to Chengdu, I expected to use the HSBC bank accounts that I have held in Shanghai for the last 5 years to do my banking. However I was told that this was not possible, so I had to open new accounts in Chengdu. (Perhaps they get 'commission' for every account opened!)

When I go to the Chengdu bank to undertake this process, I always try to use the same person, showing her the previous receipts and telling her it's just the same as last time, hoping that maybe it will be a little quicker. But no, every time it seems like a brand-new adventure!! So she (Vicky Tan is her name) eventually gave me the new receipt saying the money had been transferred to pounds and so I went back to work and immediately transferred the pounds to my Cheltenham HSBC account. A few minutes later I had a call from Vicky saying that she had made a mistake, and could I transfer all the money back to the Chinese currency account. Well, I told her it was too late and the money was already sitting without any problem in my UK account. Apparently she had hit the wrong button on the computer and transferred the Rmb in Chengdu to the multi-currency account in Shanghai, this she was not allowed to do. With tongue in cheek, I said that if she was not allowed to do it how would the sophisticated Chinese banking system allow it to happen? The cheap sarcasm was lost on the distressed Vicky, so I asked to speak to the manager, saying that there was no way I was going to transfer money back and risk another two sets of exchange losses and goodness knows what other risks. She said she would talk to her manager and call me back. This she did about an hour later, saying that they had managed to solve the problem without moving the money around the world, but I would need to sign another lot of documents so please could I come into the bank again today. The factory is about a 45-minute drive from the bank and since I was at work, I said that this was not possible. The poor girl was obviously being pressurised by her boss to get it sorted before the end of the day so Vicky asked if she could meet me after work to sign the documents. (There's an offer I don't get every day!!) Well, we eventually met outside my apartment block at 6.30pm to sign several papers that probably saved her from getting the sack, and all because of the restrictive Chinese banking system.

I hope I don't get injured over the next few days before I leave to come home. I'm sure it's the thought that I've only got limited time here that makes me view some of the difficulties with newfound anger rather than meek acceptance. The big one that really gets the Mr. Angry in me coming out is not being able to cross the road when there is the green man light at pedestrian crossings, showing it's safe to cross. China, much like the USA and France, allows cars to turn right (like a left-hand turn in the UK) at junctions even if there is a red light, as long as the road is clear. So I regularly find myself standing at a pedestrian crossing waiting for the red man to turn green, and when it does I start to cross the road, only to find that cars are now coming at me from my left-hand side. They obviously feel that they have the right of way and force the pedestrians to jump back to let them through. Well not me, I've turned into 'Mr. Angry' and stand there, daring them to run me over, and when they get close, I hit the car with my fist, point at the green light and shout some obscenity. Yes, I've got a few bruises on my arms and hands to show for it. I know that I am legally in the right but as ever the police don't care, and all the Chinese just accept that it's not worth the risk fighting a moving vehicle and so the wrong just continues. I know I'm fighting a losing battle, but it feels good to make a stand against the arrogance of the Chinese drivers, and also it offsets some of the other traffic difficulties I encounter for which I can do nothing.

I've now got my new part-time contract in place which moves me into semi-retirement mode for several months, although the actual length of time will depend on how the businesses develop. My next trip back to China will be for the first two weeks of June because it is the end of the company's financial year so there will be lots to sort out. But I can probably handle a couple of weeks of pig's bits, pollution and crazy traffic, knowing that I will be back within a matter of days to good ol' Blighty. Even if it is to a new government stating lots of ambitious things but in reality changing virtually nothing!!

Looking back at the last 18 months it has been quite frustrating from a business point of view because the key customers have suffered from the clampdown on Chinese corruption and the general slowdown in China. This has had a direct knock-on to our business, putting the expected growth back at least one year. However, the good news is that it has started to pick up over the last few weeks. From a living point of view it has been a more 'ex-patty' type of existence than I have had in other Chinese cities, which my current waistline can certainly testify to, and I've made quite a few new friends who no doubt will visit the UK sometime in the future. But when all is said and done the time has come to get back to my 'normal' life and I'm looking forward to seeing you all very soon.

Best wishes to you all, and by the way the answer is Queen Mary,
Ma Ding.

CHINA STORIES – Part-time working – June 2015-present

The move to part-time working or semi-retirement at the age of nearly 60 has been one of the best decisions I've ever made, I would recommend it to everyone. A Brit called Dean, who has been with me in China for about 8 months in the position of Engineering Manager and who was responsible for putting the large machine tools in the new factory, has been appointed as the new General Manager. I support him with two or three Skype calls a week and then every couple of months I travel back to Chengdu for about 10 days to keep a close watch on the business, help Dean with any problems and ensure the key customer relationships are maintained. I've even given Dean a bit of finance training from a simpleton's point of view, he now understands nearly as much as I do (which isn't a lot, but pretty good for a couple of engineers!); as far as the UK bosses are concerned they seem to be more than happy for me to support the business in China which lets them focus on other issues. I obviously report back to the bosses on a regular basis.

One aspect of this new role is that the regular emails to friends and relatives regaling various stories is now a thing of the past, since I am able to meet up back home and bore folks face-to-face with any stories I may have following my latest visit to China. So for this part of my 'China career' I'll just report the main events.

THE CITY OF CHENGDU

It's probably worth saying a few words about the city where I lived as a resident for the best part of two years and would spend several weeks a year on and off until the end of 2019.

Situated in the west of China, just south of Tibet, it has its own very distinct history and culture. It is a very old city, with an ancient population called the Shu who inhabited the area over 3000 years ago and made incredible bronze masks and other artefacts which can be seen in the local museums. The city has around 17 million people today and although that's well in excess of London, I never felt that it was huge, primarily due to the layout and very user-friendly public transport system. The city is laid out like a bicycle wheel with the central hub being Tianfu Plaza and roads emanating out from it. The main north/south road being Renmin Lu (People's Road), and then there are several ring roads, numbered from 1 to 4, with the first about 1km from the centre and each other about another kilometre further out. My original apartment was just south of the 2nd ring road and very close to Renmin South Road, so about 6.30 on a clock face.

As usual in China adding critical infrastructure is a priority compared to people's living areas and the 2nd ring road is now the main thoroughfare for getting around the city. It is a double decker road with dedicated bus lanes all the way round and for most of the orbit has 3 lanes for cars and taxis. I use the bus on a regular basis since the fares are really cheap (about 30p a ride, even for a complete circuit!).

Underneath all this is the metro system. When I first moved to Chengdu there were only 2 lines; Line 1 which was the north/south line basically running under People's Road, and line 2 which went from east to west, with both lines intersecting at Tianfu Plaza (the hub). Now after only a few years there are 10 lines including a circular line covering most areas of the city as well as the airport and train stations. Both the metro and overground stations have 'airport like' security screening for passengers and their bags, with police looking on constantly! Very reassuring!

Most of the signage around the city (road signs, places of interest, metro and bus stations, etc.) is in English as well as Chinese making it very easy for the visitor to get to where they're going.

There are also several parks of various sizes spread around the city, so although the main streets, shopping areas and transport systems are very noisy and busy at all hours of the day and night, peaceful refuge can be sought in the parks. As long as the out of tune vocalists are avoided!

NEW ACCOMMODATION AND SUSTENANCE

As I'd given up my apartment it was now necessary to find a suitable hotel that would be comfortable enough for my regular couple of weeks in Chengdu, allow me to get to the factory fairly easily and also enable me to meet up with some old friends on occasion. Initially this was fairly easy, since Dean, the new General Manager, lived pretty close to my old apartment so I found a couple of reasonably priced hotels nearby so that the company driver, the dreaded Mr Slow, could pick me up and drop me off en route to Dean's.

Eating, however, was another issue. I've never been one to eat alone in a hotel restaurant, I find it embarrassing and often quite expensive for average food. Although one of the hotel rooms I occasionally used did have a small kitchenette, the hotel was often fully booked and quite expensive for a company not making much money. So in the end it was necessary to eat in the factory canteen at lunchtimes and find something else for the evenings.

It's worth saying a few words about the factory canteen: early on, as we were getting the new factory up and running, we gave each employee about a pound a day to cover their midday meal. So most brought something in from outside and if necessary used the microwave to heat it up. However, it soon became more efficient for the company to provide a meal for all who wanted it. When the factory was set up, we employed a married couple (English names: Steven and Anna) in their mid-fifties to act as security guard and cleaner. They lived on site in a small one-room facility joined to the guardhouse. So we gave Anna a sum of money each week to provide a hot meal for about 25 of us. If the meals were of appropriate quality, then everybody would be happy and if Anna could make a little out of the deal then she was also happy. As you would probably expect the first few months were pretty good and everyone was reasonably happy. Dean and I would also be OK with some form of meat or fish, tofu, veg and rice. Then there was a bit of deterioration, not in the quantity, but particularly in the meat, which from my point of view was just bits of gristle and bone. So words were had. Then Chinese ingenuity came in. Steven and Anna then started to cultivate the unconcreted land surrounding the factory; a strip about 1 metre wide and probably 250 metres long on 3 sides of the factory. Suddenly all sorts of vegetables and some fruits started sprouting up (in most areas of China there are 2 growing seasons a year) which helped offset some of the costs so that meat became edible again and fresh fruit was provided for pud.

My evening meals were a real mixture; from going out with Dean for a proper meal to buying some pasta thing such as ravioli or tortellini from the French Carrefour supermarket and heating it up in my hotel room kettle. Luvely!

BACK TO BUSINESS

The business started to improve as the volumes picked up a bit and we found some new customers. But then the Chinese Central Government decided that all capital equipment (such as MRI scanners) bought for state-owned companies, such as hospitals, must be purchased from Chinese businesses. So this caused a problem with our two main customers; one was German and the other partly owned by USA shareholders. So, unfortunately just as we were beginning to see our way to profitable growth we were kicked back. One of the customers (where we had the operations within their factory) frantically started to restructure by removing any foreign influence and trying to attract new Chinese investors. All this took time and whilst this was happening our sales reduced. The German-owned customer would then only rely on their 'supposedly superior German technology' to get sales in China together with increased export volumes from their Chinese factory in Shenzhen. So the businesses limped along and we kept our costs tightly controlled. It has to be said that the team in China were very loyal and supportive with very few leavers during this difficult period.

However, by March 2016 Dean decided that he had experienced enough of the fun in China and that as his Chinese secondment contract came to an end he was relocated back to the UK. This left us trying to find a new General Manager. As luck would have it, one of the managers who worked for me in Changzhou back in 2011, and subsequently worked for my new UK boss when he was the Divisional Director of David Brown, was looking for a new role. His name was Sun Gang, known to us as George, a purchasing and logistics specialist who spoke good English and was very trustworthy. If we were to employ this person, he would need support to be a General Manager. On the basis of better the devil you know, particularly in China, I was asked if I would continue in my support role so we could appoint George as the new General Manager. This I agreed to, and George and I have worked very well together over the last few years. I visited *every* two-three months and we talk on the phone nearly *every* other day. What many people forget is that working as a boss of a remote subsidiary company is a very lonely existence, particularly if your home and family are not close by. I have experienced this for many years so understand what it's like to be making decisions in isolation, with poor communication with the parent company, particularly when there is an eight-hour time difference. For George, his family and home are in Shanghai, a three-hour flight away, so he was very much on his own in Chengdu. My regular communication with him was critical for his wellbeing and success.

George rented a small apartment close to the factory so we did away with the company driver and I had to find a different hotel that would enable me to commute to the factory but still offer the possibility of getting to meet old friends at weekends.

George proved very capable of finding new sales opportunities as our reputation for high quality manufacturing to stringent 'German' standards became well known. Also his experience of ensuring the right type of quality suppliers at the right price started to put the business on the road to sustainable profitability. On my regular visits I would be wheeled out as the 'expert foreigner' to give new customers confidence that there was significant technical support from the UK. Business performance and prospects during the period 2017-2019 were all looking good ... but then the Wuhan Flu (COVID 19) arrived ...

THE NEW CHINA ACQUISITION –
Kunshan 2017

The British parent company that I worked for sold off their aerospace parts division after making it more profitable and decided to buy an old British company called Hayward Tyler which designed and manufactured large pumps. It is a company I had known for many years since it was a customer of the company that I first started working for in 1978; there really isn't much new in this world! With this acquisition, with large factories in Luton, England and Vermont, USA, came a small subsidiary company in Kunshan, China. Kunshan is situated about 1 hour by car west of Shanghai. The business also had a sales and service office in the centre of Shanghai. The Chinese business was really a service and repair capability for the original Hayward Tyler equipment manufactured in either the UK or the USA and installed in Chinese power stations. The sales staff in China were trying to sell new Hayward Tyler pumps to the many new power stations that were being built in China every year. However, the same problem that we had in Chengdu occurred when the Chinese government stated that new capital equipment must be purchased from Chinese companies, or at least manufactured in China. So the previous owners of Hayward Tyler agreed to a multi-million pound project to build a brand new factory with all the capability to design and manufacture these large pumps in China. Contracts had been agreed by the time that my British company bought Hayward Tyler, and when the UK bosses started looking at some of the detail they were concerned at the overall cost of the investment.

Since I was a regular visitor to China it was felt that I could help oversee this project and maybe cut some of the costs. So early in 2017 I would fly in to Shanghai, be picked up and driven to Kunshan where I would go through the details of the new factory project with the local project manager, agree priorities, cost savings and timing plan. I would then fly over to Chengdu to carry on with my normal duties. It soon became apparent that this new factory project was based on a wish list as if there were no financial constraints, and as soon as I started digging into the details I found loads of money that could be either saved or deferred. I was not that popular with the local General Manager, a lady called Mary Song, who clearly saw me questioning her judgement on this project. I had a few suspicions that some of the contractors and suppliers for major elements might not have been chosen for their best value to the company, if you know what I mean! About the same time a service engineer from the USA was visiting a Chinese customer with a couple of the Hayward Tyler Chinese service engineers to sort out a potential problem. When the American guy returned to the USA, he informed the Managing Director of Hayward Tyler (an American based in Vermont) that the Chinese service engineers were telling him some stories and rumours concerning possible corruption in the Chinese business, particularly on behalf of the GM, Mary Song. By this time, mid-summer, I had visited Kunshan several times and had built a reasonable relationship with some of the staff, so I was asked to surreptitiously do some investigation to see if any of the allegations were true. Not an easy task!

So during my next visit to Kunshan I made an excuse to look at and understand the accounts and staff structure, supposedly to understand the return on the project investment. When I started digging down it became apparent that some questions could not be answered without indicating that there were indeed some potential areas of corruption. So I fed this back to the bosses and they decided to fly out to Kunshan and suspend the GM. Obviously the business still needed to be managed so they asked me to fill in as full-time General Manager for about 3 months. This I agreed to do as long as I could still support the Chengdu businesses by going there for a couple of days each month. Also, could I find someone to do a full investigation of the potential corruption in the company? Luckily the finance manager that I recruited for the Joint Venture based in Changzhou back in 2010 and who I then brought in to the Hangzhou business in 2012 was available to help and lived about a 2-hour train journey from Kunshan. So she came in on an interim basis and together we peeled back the onion on what transpired to be a very broad range of issues. So a very busy, but interesting few months!

Without going into too much detail what we discovered was corruption on a huge scale to the personal benefit of Mary and her family costing the company significant amounts. Mary was very quickly fired, and all of the obvious issues corrected but others still needed careful investigation. For me one of the biggest issues was why were the previous UK-based management and their local auditors not able to pick up these problems? They seem to have been so ignorant of Chinese business methods and were letting Mary run things without questioning her or doing any checks. For your interest the main areas of corruption were: putting some of her relatives on the payroll so they received a salary but did not appear on the premises or ever do any work for the company; giving her husband a very expensive electric car and insurances funded by the company; paying various friends/relatives for contracts that were either way above market value or just not done; manipulating her own salary and expenses to avoid paying tax; and getting some customer jobs done at the weekend, 'off the books', so she could personally get the payment and then she would pay the workers involved cash.

I could go on, but in the end we had to get the business back on an even keel, move into the new factory, and set up for the future with a new General Manager.

We moved into the new factory as planned, the machines and equipment and materials all in place; however, initially there were no offices, so we hired a couple of 40ft containers and put these against an outside wall inside the factory, cut some windows in them and installed some air conditioning. One container for the engineering team and purchasing, the other for management (myself), finance and the operations manager. It sounds pretty grim, but it wasn't too bad, and we could see the permanent offices being built. After a few weeks it all settled down and the employees helped get the new facilities established whilst continuing their normal jobs, we cancelled all of Mary's spurious contracts and found new service suppliers as required. I did spend a lot of time building the management team and so obviously had to hold several team meals, and karaoke sessions!!

After three months the UK bosses found a permanent General Manager from within the Hayward Tyler senior management team, so I spent a couple of weeks handing over the reins and then returned to the UK and looked forward to continuing the part-time support for the Chengdu businesses.

COVID TIMES

My last trip to China before Covid hit was in November 2019 and I had already booked flights and hotel for a visit to Chengdu at the end of January 2020. However, news of the Covid outbreak taking hold in China and the possibility of it spreading throughout the world made me cancel the trip. And then came lockdown, both in China and the UK. Our factories in China were shut down for several weeks, staff were stuck at home, suppliers couldn't deliver, and neither could we to our customers. Unlike the UK there was no government support for individuals or companies, so although we continued to pay our employees, we had no sales. It took several weeks to get through the first of many lockdowns and business interruptions over the next couple of years and although things settled down towards the end of 2021 China chose to isolate itself from foreign visitors so I could only support George and his team by conference calls.

At the beginning of 2022 we were approached by one of our suppliers based near Shanghai who wanted to buy our business so that he could support new customers in Sichuan province. The UK bosses were happy to pursue this opportunity to sell a business that, in truth, had never achieved its potential and had lost money during the Covid period. As ever, negotiations of this sort in China were never going to be easy, particularly as we couldn't travel to China to speak to the buyer, lawyers and others involved in the sale process. Although we agreed the structure of the deal fairly quickly, it took many months to get through the process and satisfy the Chinese authorities and conclude the deal. For my part I was finally allowed to travel to China in April 2023. I had to get a new business visa, obtain Covid PCR tests, health declarations, fingerprints, and facial recognition details in order to enter the country. I was taking all the sale contracts, side letters and debt waiver agreements for the Chinese buyers to sign.

So after three and a half years I was finally back in China. I didn't get the opportunity to visit Chengdu because I needed to meet with the new buyers whose company was based a couple of hours south of Shanghai. Also I needed to assure some of our customers that the new owners would continue to supply quality products to their businesses. I did make the time to meet up with some of my Chinese mates, have some really tasty, and not so tasty, Chinese meals, including some fish stomach! I also had a couple of free days in Shanghai so decided to go to the Natural History Museum which was near my hotel. As ever with some of the best museums in China this was extremely well put together with some great dinosaurs and an African safari landscape amongst other exhibits. I also managed to find a chocolate museum on Nanjing Road which was everything a choco-holic like me could ask for, including life-size chocolate statues of Michelangelo's David and the Venus de Milo. Sneaking some free samples it was a great way to end this visit to China!

But which one is the dinosaur!

Michelangelo would be so proud.

Our Chengdu-based companies finally got transferred to the new owners at the end of May 2023 and my work for the British company Avingtrans came to an end. However, last I heard the new Chinese boss, Mr Shen, would like to use me from time to time to help with specialist sourcing from outside China, visiting potential new customers both in Europe, and supporting when required in China. So although the work will not be as regular as my previous role, I will still be keeping my brain cell active and continue to use my unique Chinese accent to the amusement of both Chinese and English speakers alike.

A few thoughts on my Chinese language ability ...

I have always tried to learn a few words of any country that I've visited much to the embarrassment of my family when I try to use them and then the locals reply in perfect English.

I did however master French in my 30s and was fluent enough to run a business both in all four language skills; speech, listening, reading and writing. Twenty years on my brain was clearly not as capable and the Chinese language is a totally different proposition, there being no obvious link between the written word and the sound. Anyway, during my second assignment to China I decided I should really try to learn the language. Luckily there has been for a few years a halfway house between the Chinese character as written and the sound required in mandarin. This system is called Pinyin and was developed to allow a phonetics of western keyboard to bring up a choice of Chinese characters that have the similar sound. For example the Chinese for hello is , the Pinyin for this is 'ni hao', pronounced 'Knee How'. The words literally mean 'you good' but is the Chinese greeting equivalent to the western Hello.

I decided to focus my learning on conversation and the occasional use of writing short emails or texts. I downloaded the 'simplified' Chinese character set to my computer and phone. The simplified character set is now used in preference to the traditional characters which are far more complex and therefore don't lend themselves so easily to digital displays etc.

But what about the tones I hear you say! Yes it's true, mandarin does have four tones which can be used to change the basic sound to give four separate meanings. For example the basic sound 'yu' with an up tone means fish, with a down-up tone means rain, with a flat tone means silt, and with down tone means jade. I have to admit that my use of tones is pathetic but I did find that the context usually helped.

292

I remember ordering fish soup 'yu tang' in a Chinese restaurant only for the waitress to give me a funny look. Apparently I had ordered rain soup, but because we were in a restaurant she soon realised what I was trying to say since jade and silt soup were also probably not on today's menu. You don't have to get it perfectly right to communicate.

I also found a simple way of expressing the past and future by using phrases like next week or tomorrow, yesterday or last month, then saying what I was or will be doing.

The family is vitally important in China so there are many more words for different family members. For example, the elder sister is "jie jie' the younger sister is 'mei mei', elder brother 'ge ge' and younger brother 'di di'. The word for small is 'xiao' and unfortunately in one conversation when I described my small younger brother as a vicar, using the phrase 'xiao di di' there was a decided hush from all around. Little did I know that 'xiao di di' is another term for a man's willy. So you can imagine the looks I received when telling people that my willy is a vicar!! The joys of language!

The following is a short list of some of the words and phrases that I found helpful communicating in Chinese and often amazed/confused the locals when I nearly got it right!

Chinese	Pinyin	Literal meaning	Actual use
再见	zai jian	again meet	goodbye
干杯	gan bei	dry glass	cheers
明白	ming bai	bright white	I understand
大鼻子	da bize	big nose	foreigner
啤酒	pi jiu	beer	beer
火车	huo che	fire vehicle	train
出租车	chu zu che	go rent vehicle	taxi
飞机	fei ji	fly machine	plane
手机	shou ji	hand machine	mobile phone
电脑	dian nao	electric brain	computer
听不懂	ting bu dong	hear no understand	don't understand
东西	dong xi	east west	stuff/thing. Used when you don't know the word.
就点	jiu dian	alcohol shop	hotel
红酒	hong jiu	red alcohol	red wine
那个	na ge	that	a word used to fill gaps, to give you time to think, much like our 'um' and the French word 'donc'.

There are obviously many others words and phrases that follow a certain type of logic, but also many that don't. In any event I am so pleased that I took the trouble to learn as much as I did since it allowed my experience of my time in China to be so much more fulfilling.

Pray for a good deal.

Spot the English Gent.

Soon to go bust.

I think they mean carp.

Its easier if you take it out.

No wonder the chef looks pained.

A bit bright.

A very shiny set of wheels.

Who suggests these shop names?

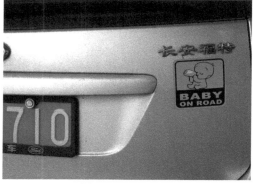

'I hope the baby's OK!'.

FINAL THOUGHTS

I consider myself to have been very fortunate to have experienced first-hand the rapid changes in this huge country, and it's had an enormous impact on me both professionally and personally. China's development over the past few years has not come without several significant problems and I suspect that the continuation of this growth will need to be very carefully managed as China takes on a more significant global role.

For the main part my involvement has been to bring modern western business practices to traditional Chinese-based businesses, trying to meld the best of both worlds; the tight controls and efficiency drives of the West together with the complex network of relationships, flexibility and speed of the East. I vividly remember an early experience as the 'big boss' when I suggested that we should consider changing some of the notice boards in the factory. One of the Chinese senior managers took this as an instruction and by the time I arrived for work the next day these changes had already happened. Thereafter I was very careful about suggesting anything! This cultural trait of 'get on and do it now, and if we have to make some changes later then we will' can be seen in many aspects of Chinese life. They set targets for things to be done, buildings completed, new railways built, etc. and will invariably deliver on time and to budget. However, often remedial action is required soon after completion, by which time the success has been publicised and the next major project declared. In the West we tend to mull things over until we think we have got the perfect plan, then eventually start, by which time the original premise has probably changed. I'm not sure which method is more effective, but it certainly is more exciting working the Chinese way and you can see that this is the attitude that is driving the country forward.

It's very easy to get bogged down discussing the difference of things like food, driving standards and the language, and no doubt, they are very interesting to compare; however, these are really only minor differences. It's also worth noting that things I found very odd in the early years in China, such as the lurid coloured cars and certain foods, have now started to be available in the UK as China extends its reach. It is however worth considering some of the similarities between our two cultures and also some of the aspects that made my time in China so rewarding. China has a wonderful history stretching back many thousands of years. In Britain we tend to start our history with the civilizing influence of the Romans about two thousand years ago. In China, several hundred years before the Romans invaded Britain Confucius was teaching his philosophy and around the same time Lao Zi was developing Taoism (sometimes called Daoism). Also the incredible terracotta army of the emperor Qin Shi Huang in Xian is from 200BC, not forgetting the early development of gunpowder and delicate porcelain (which we tend to call 'china'). I really enjoyed visiting the many impressive museums in various cities in China; from the enormous Shanghai Museum in People's Square, which took several visits to cover all the exhibitions, to the very moving museum in Nanjing commemorating the massacre by the invading Japanese army in 1937. I found the culture of friendships and business relationships relatively easy to fit in to and now have many Chinese friends who I have known for many years. I noticed early on that the Chinese sense of humour is very similar to our British one, utilizing sarcasm, irony and plays on words. Several times in meetings with different nationalities I would be laughing with the Chinese whilst the Germans or Americans wouldn't have got the joke. The Chinese sense of fun helped during some of the tough times, although the dreaded Karaoke bar can be a mixed blessing! I have been lucky enough to have visited, and worked in, many countries around the world, and I have to say that nowhere have I felt safer when I am out walking, or travelling on my own than in China, whether it be big cities or even remote villages.

However China is changing. Some of the cultural aspects

I noticed and admired when I first worked in China are now under threat: Many individuals now leave their families to travel to where the work is, only returning for festivals like the Chinese New Year. This in turn is putting the reliance on the family under pressure, with older relatives not able to be cared for by family members, so putting more strain on the already stretched (and expensive) health care system. China's aging population has caused a revision of the single child policy because there are not enough people working to support the rising pension and care costs. However, when I talk to normal people about having a second child, most now can't afford it with the increased property prices and education costs. The wealth created in recent years has not been equitable, which is now causing a rise in crime, particularly in the larger cities, and the strain of a supposedly more developed society has led to higher levels of personal stress. Although most of these impacts are being talked about openly there is no easy solution and the impact of the Covid pandemic has only added to the problems. I await with interest to see if the Chinese government can find a balanced solution whilst also tackling the climate, environmental and international trade issues. They have many thousands of years of heritage and experience to call on.

I hope the previous pages have given you a flavour of the experience that has accompanied me over the last few years. Working in China has been a third of my working life and although China has become much more self-reliant in most areas and continues to develop its own capabilities, particularly in technology, I still feel that from time-to-time an old grey-haired westerner can bring an air of confidence to commercial meetings and business efficiency, and as such I could still find myself with a role to play!!

Milton Keynes UK
Ingram Content Group UK Ltd.
UKHW022212111223
434194UK00011B/94